The
Yorkshire
Beer
Bible

3rd
EDITION

A drinker's guide to all the brewers and beers of God's own country

Simon Jenkins

GREAT NORTHERN

Great Northern Books Limited
PO Box 1380, Bradford, BD5 5FB
www.greatnorthernbooks.co.uk

Every effort has been made to acknowledge correctly and
contact the copyright holders of material in this book. Great
Northern Books apologises for any unintentional errors or
omissions, which should be notified to the publisher.

ISBN: 978-1-914227-52-3

Design and layout: David Burrill

CIP Data

A catalogue for this book is available from the British Library

MIX
Paper | Supporting
responsible forestry
FSC® C016779
www.fsc.org

A walk with the author

Yorkshire Beer Bible author Simon Jenkins hosts
regular walking tours in Leeds, where you can learn
about some local history and heritage – and call in
for drinks at one or two of his favourite pubs. Visit
the website itsthebeertalking.co.uk or scan the QR
code for details of forthcoming events.

Introduction

THE last edition of this book, published in 2019, questioned whether we were nearing 'peak beer' – whether drinkers' thirst for endless novelty might soon be satisfied, or if the stream of new breweries emerging would eventually saturate the marketplace.

At that point no-one foresaw the existential threat to the whole industry wrought by a global pandemic which stopped the hospitality industry dead in its tracks. In the space of a few short weeks, the question for breweries became less about whether to create a 7% gooseberry porter and more about how they might stay afloat.

On my many visits to breweries around Yorkshire over the past year, I've learned much about how businesses responded to these unprecedented circumstances and the many ways they adapted to survive.

Those with canning and bottling lines and healthy supermarket contracts were perhaps best insulated against the sudden closure of the on-trade. Others were forced to rapidly change tack, building on-line shopping websites, offering carry-out services from the brewery, and establishing new partnerships to package their beer. Some took Government support; many had to furlough staff.

That so many came through – albeit on a wing and a prayer – is huge testament to their ingenuity and determination, and speaks volumes for their customers' loyalty to locally-brewed, crafted Yorkshire beer. Kirkstall Brewery owner Steve Holt, told me: "The pandemic was extremely troubling for us because we're very much focused on the on-trade. There was very little assistance for breweries and if you weren't in the off-trade, you struggled."

Kirkstall invested in canning, did contract brewing for others, but even so had to take out a Government loan to help them through. "It was a tough time, and if it had gone on much longer it could have been carnage. And of course we have seen a lot of brewers who simply haven't made it through."

Of the 200 or so Yorkshire brewers featured in the 2019 edition, only 150 were still trading four years later. And – just as Covid-19 seemed almost arbitrary in who it affected the most – we have lost wonderful small producers as well as mighty beasts like Leeds and Sheffield Breweries.

While each of these closures represents a personal story for the brewers and their staff – and usually an unhappy one – some still feel more shocking than others.

I'd been so impressed by Spotlight Brewing, a fabulous social enterprise employing adults with learning difficulties and using the beers to raise awareness of some of their life-limiting conditions. I also had a soft spot for tiny Hungry Bear in Meanwood, Leeds, with their label-less swing-top bottles and imaginative ales curated by talented brewer Phil Marsh. We have also been robbed of the wonderfully-constructed beers and beautiful slender bottles of Scarborough's Asylum Harbour. I had high hopes for Bradford wheat beer specialist Eyes, and was really sad to learn that my old friend Katie Marriott had called time on Nomadic too. A fuller list of those we have lost over these turbulent four years can be found on page 222.

The pressures of the cost-of-living crisis may be different, but are no less a threat to those breweries that remain, as Steve Holt explains:

"There are rapidly rising costs of production, both in the raw materials and in utility prices, while the consumer's spending power is also being squeezed. I've seen recessions in the past and the beer industry usually weathers these pretty well, but this time it could be different. No-one really knows how this is going to play out."

We're talking in Brownhill and Co, a craft beer bar in the centre of Leeds, where a couple of his beers are being served on draught. And here Steve admits that while he'd like to see Kirkstall beers offered more widely, he's wary that customer perceptions may put a further brake on any expansion plans. "It's all very well having national aspirations but that can be very hard to maintain in a competitive market. Take the likes of Brewdog, Beavertown, Camden: what was crafted beer a few years ago has become mainstream. Brewdog went from being a trendy craft product to being so completely in the mainstream that you just won't find it in places like this."

And as we go to press, the news that local legends Black Sheep have been placed into administration is a further sign that even the biggest players in the local market have struggled in these uniquely challenging times.

But remarkably, through this period of attrition for our industry a trickle

KIRKSTALL
BREWERY

At **Kirkstall Brewery**, our Revival Series of Prize Ales draws upon the heritage of our predecessors The Kirkstall Brewery Company (1834-1983), recreating beers from the 1930s, 1920s and even right back to the 1880s.

Our Prize Ales form not just a link to the past, but also a source of inspiration for our future. Visit our website to find out more and look out for a Prize Ale on the bar near you.

KIRKSTALLBREWERY

WWW.KIRKSTALLBREWERY.COM

of new contenders have emerged. Some were already in the embryonic phase before the pandemic, others forged their business model to suit the lockdown world, and are growing from there. More than 30 breweries are making their first appearance in the book – from the tiny Barker's, established during lockdown in a Huddersfield back garden, to the exciting Tartarus, who in just three years have grown from a suburban cellar to take over the sizeable brewkit vacated by the rapidly expanding North Brewing. Newbies DMC are bringing a host of interesting ginger beers to the market, while the closure of the much-loved Hop Studio has opened the way for Another Beer to scale up from cuckoo brewing.

As with the two previous editions of the *Yorkshire Beer Bible*, I set out with the intention of including every single commercial brewery in the county. Though I found 180, it's clear that new breweries are opening all the time, so it's very likely that some – the newest certainly, but even some older, smaller brewers – might have slipped through the net. For that I apologise.

And somehow, miraculously, the Yorkshire brewing scene seems as diverse and exciting as ever. And optimistic too, even as the costs of production spiral upwards and the storm-clouds of a global recession seem to gather on the horizon. So many of those I spoke to continue to trade with imagination and confidence; many credited the loyalty of their customers with redoubling their efforts, and galvanising their determination to pull through.

And, despite the best efforts of Covid-19, the Yorkshire brewing scene is as varied, vibrant and vigorous as ever.

Happy drinking!

Simon Jenkins June 2023

3 Non Beards

Rook and Gaskill, 12 Laurence Street, York, YO10 3WP; T: 07980 994210;
W: www.rookandgaskillyork.co.uk

York's lovely old Rook and Gaskill pub, named after two local sheep rustlers hanged in the 17th century, is home to this one-barrel brewery, established just a few months before the start of the pandemic.

Facial hair is a recurring theme in brewing, so the name celebrates the fact that friends and founders Andy Aspin, Paul Marshall and Jason Simpson have just one moustache between them. Paul is landlord at the Rook, and can now serve his own beers on the bar. Early brews included the American pale ale **Misty Mountain Hop** (4.2%) – one of the trio is clearly a Led Zeppelin fan – and vanilla porter **Trade Winds** (4.7%). But the only one I've caught up with so far is the easy-going red ale **Running Red Lights** (5%) whose toffee and biscuit notes are sharpened by some red berry juiciness. It was a big hit at the York Beer Festival in 2022.

1086 Brewery

The Old Brewhouse, Cusworth Lane, Doncaster, DN5 7TU; T: 01302 639880;
🅕 🅞 @1086brewery

Established just after the previous edition of the *Yorkshire Beer Bible* went to press, 1086 occupies the original brewhouse of Grade I listed Cusworth Hall. An on-site taproom is the ideal place to try beers such as the pale amber **Cuzeuuorde** (4.3%) and the easy-drinking, biscuity best bitter **Lady Isabella** (4.5%).

1086 was the year of the Domesday Book, by which time Norman baron Roger de Busli, who had taken part in the conquest two decades before, had been rewarded with huge tracts of land in Nottinghamshire, Derbyshire and Yorkshire. He is remembered in the gently malty and sessionable **Roger of Bully** (3.9%).

Abbeydale Brewery

Unit 8, Aizlewood Road, Sheffield, S8 0YX; T: 0114 281 2712;
E: info@abbeydalebrewery.co.uk; W: abbeydalebrewery.co.uk;
🅕 *@abbeydalebrewery;* 𝕏 📷 *@abbeydalebeers.*

South of the city centre, well away from the craft heartland of the S3 postcodes, Abbeydale is Sheffield's biggest brewer. The sad – and thankfully temporary – closure of Kelham Island in 2022 briefly bestowed upon it further status as Sheffield's oldest, Abbeydale having ticked past the quarter-century mark during the pandemic.

It is named to honour Beauchief Abbey which thrived and brewed here until the ravages of the dissolution. Kirkstall Brewery is another which preserves an ancient monastic name.

A major expansion in 2018 annexed a neighbouring unit with more than £200,000 spent on new vessels, a malt milling system and laboratory equipment enabling a 20% increase in capacity, and the potential for their own events space. During Covid, this was followed by a £75,000 investment in a new canning line to cope with the spike in home drinking.

More than half of production is given over to the golden **Moonshine** (4.3%) – a bronze medallist at 2018's Champion Beer of Britain awards, while another regular is the amiably grapefruity New Zealand pale ale **Deception** (4.1%), a former Sheffield Beer of the Year.

After years of being brewed in changing batches, each focused on a single hop, the IPA **Serenity** (3.8%) has now settled down to a reliably bitter recipe of Cascade and Galaxy. Their straight-up traditional bitter **Daily Bread** (3.8%) and crisp lager **Heresy** (4.5%) maintain the liturgical theme.

While cask beer remains their focus, Abbeydale have long been adopters of canning – amongst those packaged this way is the strong dark **Black Mass** (6.66%) whose name and beastly strength speak to the sinister side of their ecclesiastical roots; an online shop services a thirsty trade.

Abbeydale's restless enthusiasm for experimentation is perhaps best illustrated by their ever-evolving Brewers Emporium range, covering all manner of styles. The Funk Dungeon is a further innovative, small-batch

barrel project, exploring barrel ageing, souring and mixed fermentation techniques. The Sheffield Indie Beer Feast in March 2023 provided an opportunity to try several newcomers including the intense juice bomb IPA **Cloud Peak** (4.8%) and indulgent imperial stout **Indulgence** (10.6%). Even so, amid this elegant lathering of flavour, I was most struck by the cloudy, refreshing, revivifying nature of the gentle table beer **Restoration** (2.8%).

Abbeydale's single pub, the Rising Sun in Fulwood – and the current Sheffield CAMRA pub of the year – is perhaps the best place to make your own judgment.

🍺 Heathen (4.1%)
There is a moment, just as you prepare to take your first sip, just as your nose is filled with the wonderful heady zest of grapefruit and pineapple, that you wonder if you've picked up a can of Lilt by mistake. The liquid is the same enticing gold, both have colourful cans, and that big fruit blast just before the beer crosses the threshold has all the sunshine zing of the totally tropical taste.

And yet, as soon as it hits the palate, Heathen's hop character barges determinedly to the foreground, throwing its big bitter weight about. And though there's a little spike of carbonation, there's nothing here to match the full-on fizz of a fruity pop. Yet in the aftertaste, more of the citrus emerges in a dusty dry finish.

Heathen is styled an American pale ale, and the significant hopping is very much a trademark of the genre, though this one's moderate strength and ultimately quaffable character ensure that it remains wholly (and holy) in the mainstream.

Acorn Brewery

Unit 3 Aldham Industrial Estate, Wombwell, Barnsley, S73 8HA;
T: 01226 270734; W: acorn-brewery.co.uk; E: dave@acorn-brewery.co.uk;
🅕 *@AcornBreweryBarnsley;* 🅣 *@acornbrewery*

Dave Hughes used a redundant 10-barrel kit from a pub in the defunct Firkin chain to establish Acorn in 2003, and has since upgraded to a 25-barrel plant.

Rich and rounded chestnut-coloured **Barnsley Bitter** (3.8%), with its long bitter finish, is perhaps their best-known product, having been a Champion Beer of Britain finalist on many occasions. Others include ultra-pale session ale **Yorkshire Pride** (3.7%), a permanent bottled beer on P&O cruise ship Britannia, liquorice-accented **Old Moor Porter** (4.4%) and an **IPA** (5%) which uses a different single hop every time.

Jet-black, firmly bitter **Gorlovka** (6%) is named in honour of the Eastern Ukrainian city twinned with Barnsley – and is the Acorn take on the Imperial Stout style. It has a complex beefy taste that melds strong black coffee and dark chocolate and just a hint of coconut. A monthly-changing list of specials and seasonals complete the line-up; Barnsley beers are widely available in cask, keg and bottle.

Though no longer owned by Acorn, the brewery's former pub the Old No 7, a four-time CAMRA regional pub of the year, remains an ideal place to try their wares.

🍺 Acorn Blonde (4%)

When I held a beer tasting at Waterstone's in Leeds a while back, I began by introducing punters to this easy-drinking, crisp and refreshing pale ale – which is not a million miles from a continental lager. Acorn Blonde is very pale of colour and has a sweet, almost floral aroma, and some flowery citric notes persist into a sharp taste that buzzes around the palate with a significant amount of carbonation. The aftertaste is short-lived and faintly metallic – but as one of my Waterstone's tasters put it: "One brief encounter with this Barnsley Blonde wasn't nearly enough for me."

Ainsty Ales

Manor Farm, Acaster Malbis, YO23 2TY; T: 01904 703233;
W: ainstyales.co.uk; E: info@ainstyales.co.uk; 📘 🐦 📷 *@ainstyales*

Ainsty Ales could be the only brewhouse in Britain to have a piano in the corner, and though the daily variations of humidity and temperature have forced it well out of tune it still gets played at the weekly weekend socials at the countryside taproom.

Named after the York and Ainsty Wapentake, a medieval subdivision of the county, Ainsty Ales began brewing in York in 2014 and has won an impressive haul of regional and national industry awards.

Sharp and fruity pale ale **Angel** (3.6%) is a permanent, as is blonde **Flummoxed Farmer** (4%) their biggest-selling beer, along with **Bantam Best** (4.2%) double gold-winning American pale ale **Cool Citra** (4.4%) and oatmeal stout **Ainsty Assassin** (4.9%). New to the range in 2022 is their first pilsner-style kegged lager, **Jewel of York** (4.5%).

Aitcheson's East Yorkshire Beer

The Brick Barn, Ferry Rd, Beverley, HU7 5XY; T: 07456 063670;
W: eastyorkshirebeer.co.uk; E: steve@eastyorkshirebeer.co.uk;
f *@eastyorkshirebeer*

The closure of East Yorkshire Beer Co came early in 2020, but undeterred, brewer Steve Aitcheson moved a couple of miles down the road and started again in an old 17th-century brick shed.

"It was in a real state," he says. "But with the help of family I decided to take it on and construct a brewery to suit. But then the plague hit; I managed to get the brewery licensed and brewing enough beer to sell through Facebook in bottle and bag-in-box to the new home bar market. Fortunately this kept us going."

His new brewery appends his surname to the old name: "I didn't want to lose the domain 'East Yorkshire Beer' as it's so good for search engines, so Aitcheson's East Yorkshire Beer was born."

Several of his brews honour much-missed local pubs. **Earl De Grey** (4.5%) hails from the softer, more nuanced end of the IPA spectrum, and recalls a notorious Hull boozer whose young ladies would service the needs of visiting seamen. The Star was a popular mock Tudor pub in Hull's West Street, demolished 25 years ago for a new shopping centre. Its name is revived in the sharp, refreshing, cold-filtered German-style pilsner, **Star of the West** (4.5%) a surprisingly good, locally-brewed antidote to some of the ubiquitous big-brand lagers.

Oats and wheat lend body and texture to **Aitcheson's Cream Stout** (4.5%) while dark mild **Endike Black** (3.5%) – named after a pub now serving time as a supermarket – has won medals in the Champion Mild of Yorkshire contest in both 2022 and 2023.

Amity Brew Co *New*

Unit 15-16, Sunny Bank Mills, 83-85 Town Street, Farsley, LS28 5UJ;
T: 07572 953655; W: www.amitybrew.co; E: contact@amitybrew.co;
f 🐦 📷 *@amitybrewco*

"We opened straight into Tier Three," says Amity boss Russ Clarke, recalling how the resurgent pandemic hit the launch of the brewery in December 2020. "Our taproom was open for about half a day and then we had to close again."

Amity was founded by a group of friends with a love of great beer, led by Brewdog and North Brewing alumnus Russ. "Once the restrictions finally ended, we opened again in April 2021 and this past year has been amazing."

The rediscovery and resurgence of Sunny Bank Mills has been one of west Leeds' most remarkable stories of the past few years. Established as a textiles mill in Victorian times, it is now home to a host of businesses, an art gallery, leisure, food and drink and education spaces as well as a vast archive of fabrics and designs chronicling its rich history and the role it played in local life.

Open from Thursday to Sunday, Amity is the mill's beer garden and beautiful red-brick taproom, serving a changing selection of products such as the substantial West Coast pale ale **Sunny Bank** (6%), summer fruit sour **Cosmic Whip** (4%) and the crisp, German-malted **Festoon Helles** (4.6%).

In 2022, Amity took over wonderful city-centre alehouse Reliance to launch their first cask ale, the traditional best bitter **Red Lane** (4.2%), all gentle toffee, orange and soothing malt. Regular collaboration brews freshen up the range; plans for a barrel-aged brew underline the friends' confidence for the future.

 Water Pistol (4.6%)

New Zealand's Motueka hop is front and centre here, bringing rich juicy lime to an assertive hazy pale ale which has quickly become Amity's biggest seller. It is a crisp tropical refresher, a perfect summer beer with an aftertaste that lasts and lasts.

Ampleforth Abbey Beer

Ampleforth, York, YO62 4EY; T: 01439 766099;
W: ampleforthabbeydrinks.org.uk;
E: abbeydrinks@ampleforthabbey.org.uk;
🅕 *@ampleforthabbeydrinks;* 🅞 *@ampleforthbeer*

Fleeing France after the revolution, a community of Benedictine Monks founded Ampleforth Abbey in 1802, bringing with them the secret recipe for dark and full-bodied, spicy, biscuity Belgian Dubbel style **Ampleforth Abbey Beer** (7%). The monastic order continues to thrive, as does production of their single bottled beer, which has won a string of awards, including being named best drink in the 2012 Deliciously Yorkshire Award. The beer is now made at Little Valley Brewery; in recent times the monks have added two premium ciders to their devotions.

Another Beer *New*

Unit 3, Handley Park, Elvington, York YO41 4AR; T: 07403 264242;
W: anotherbeer.co.uk; 🅕 *@anotherbeerltd;* 🅞 *@another_beer_ltd*

The recent sad demise of the highly-regarded Hop Studio opened the way for another brewery to move into their premises on the former airbase south-east of York. Yorkshire Air Museum and the Allied Air Forces Memorial is close by.

Brummie James Fawcett began brewing in his London shed, before moving to York in 2019 and establishing Another Beer as a cuckoo brewer, supplying various venues across the city. The move to Elvington represents a significant expansion of the business, with James launching a crowdfunding initiative to support the creation of a taproom and events venue in the mezzanine of this cavernous warehouse space.

His only beer I've found so far is the delightful juice bomb **Session IPA** (3.8%), whose lime and apricot character is derived from New Zealand's Wai-Iti hop.

Anthology Brewing

Unit 6, Armley Link, Armley Road, Leeds, LS12 2QN; T: 07594 975245;
W: anthologybrewing.co.uk; E: info@anthologybrewing.co.uk;
🅕 🅧 🅘 *@anthologybrewco*

Former musician Liam Kane is the driving force behind this one-man, five-barrel operation close to Armley jail, which opened in 2019.

Drinkers' favourites like the Cardigan Arms, Whitelocks and Brudenell Social Club are early adopters of his ever-changing hop-forward pale ales such as the **New England Session Pale** (3.8%), **Dry Hopped Pale** (5%) and **US Session IPA** (4.5%). Liam also brews the house beer for Leeds's highly-regarded beer and charcuterie venue Friends of Special. Events at his on-site taproom have begun to attract a significant following, too.

The hazy and cheek-suckingly sour **Bergamot Sorbet** (4%), driven by the cleansing power of citrus, which I first encountered at Leeds International Beer Festival in autumn 2022, is emblematic of the quality and imagination behind each of Liam's beers.

★ ANTHOLOGY ★	ABV	HALF
BERGAMOT SORBET SOUR	4	3
SICILIAN LEMON PALE	4.2	3
BLUEBERRY BERLINER WEISSE	4.1	3
IPA | CITRA	6	3.5
BILLIONAIRES TO ANOTHER GALAXY	5.6	3.5
BA EXPORT STOUT	7.4	4
T SHIRTS	£16	
TOTES	£5	
PIN BADGES	£3	

Atom Brewing

Unit 4, Food & Tech Park, Malmo Road, Hull, HU7 0YF; T: 01482 820 572;
W: atombeers.com; E: drinks@atombeers.com; 🅕 🅣 🅘 *@atombeers*

"We didn't set it up to make beer," says Scotsman Allan Rice, rather knocking me sideways with the opening gambit of a conversation in his office above the brewery on the northern fringes of Hull. "Primarily we saw it as an educational outreach facility."

Allan has a degree in physiology, his wife Sarah a PhD in biochemistry, and it's their passion for science which drives Atom, an enthusiasm evident both in the names of their beers and in the regular educational sessions they lay on for students from nearby schools and colleges.

Allan recognises something of himself in the young people of Hull: "It's quite similar to my home town of Greenock. We want to inspire this next generation to understand that science can be relevant to them. Coming here they can actually use their mathematics, their chemistry, their thermodynamics, and begin to think: 'I can do this.'"

For the last year or so, the science has been in the hands of head brewer Mike Antonacci, who had spells with breweries in Germany, Sweden and back home in Italy before joining Atom on the eve of the Brexit immigration deadline. He has bought into the Atom culture, working to hone their well-established beers, while developing some new ones of his own.

The New England IPA **Stratosphere** (6.5%) typifies Atom's scientific approach. The complex recipe involves mash-hopping with Cascade – introducing hops at the very start of the brewing process – before Apollo, Citra and Centennial are used during the boil. "And, because of the name, we also have Strata as a VIP hop for this one," says Mike. He uses a special yeast strain whose enzymes release thiols – compounds bound in the malt and yeast – to give the beer a richer fruit flavour. The result is a rich tropical punch, with bags of pineapple and papaya. "I'm really proud of it," he says.

Sessionable and gluten-free West Coast IPA **Quantum State** (4.2%) has a simpler recipe and is more noticeably bitter, while Madagascan vanilla lends body and sweetness to the gentle **Binary Mixtures** stout (4.5%). Flagship American pale ale **Catalyst** (5.4%) is big on juiciness and has a pleasing mouthfeel; Citra hops drive

Dark Matter (4.5%)

It was during one of the periodic breaks from lockdown that I first got hold of a few cans of this lovely chocolate stout. While many beers in this style are a deal stronger, the clever Atom boffins have crafted a jet-black ale which belies its moderate strength to deliver bags of vibrant autumnal flavours – the crackle of woodsmoke, the bitter twang of coffee and dark chocolate, the salty sweetness of burnt toffee.

its junior relation, the tropical fruit **Prism** (4.5%).

"I'm really keen on my lagers," says Mike, introducing the pale and crisp **Venn** (4.4%) which uses Saaz hops, German malt and yeast to create as authentic a crisp central European lager. "Having started brewing in Germany, I've done a lot of work on Venn to make it as good as it could be." He's succeeded, it's a lemony Helles delight, with just a twist of ginger.

Named to honour a Pink Floyd classic, **Astronomy Domine** (12%) may be at the rocket fuel end of the range, but is actually a beautifully soporific nightcap, a complex blend of black and chocolate malts, demerara sugar and maltodextrin, liquid cacao nibs, oats and coconut.

Bad Seed Brewery

7 Rye Close, York Road Business Park, Malton, YO17 6YD;
T: 01653 695783; W: badseedbrewery. com; E: info@badseedbrewery.com;
🅕 🅨 🅞 @badseedbrewery

Bad Seed was established on an industrial estate in Malton by actor Chris Waplington who is now winning ripples of appreciative applause for his beer. His previous career is name-checked by the complex fruit punch **Stage Hand** (4.2%) whose cocktail of mango, orange and papaya is derived from liberal use of the Mosaic hop.

Much-loved hop Cascade lends a typically juicy, grapefruity influence to **Dalliance** (4%), while the pale ale **Kiwi** (3.8%) derives a headrush of zinginess from New Zealand's Wakatu hop. There's a **Session IPA** (4%) and a chocolate-rich dessert stout **Cake Hole** (5.7%) but I was most impressed by the full-on tropical assault of the West Coast-influenced **Grid Code** (5.5%).

Barker Bridge Brewery *New*

Manor Farm, Cullingworth, BD13 5HN; T: 07496 284433;
E: sales@barkerbridge.co.uk; 🎝 *@Barker Bridge Brewery;*
🐦 *@Barker_bridge;* 📷 *@barkerbridgebrewery*

Working on his family farm while considering a career in film editing, Matt Barker had a Damascene conversion on the road to a brewery. "One day I was picking up used grains from a local brewery to feed our cattle – and I suddenly started thinking. I knew Old Spot Brewery had finished brewing and I knew that the plant was still there. All that was missing were some new ideas, new recipes and a new name."

After a long chat with Old Spot's former head brewer Chris Thompson, Matt established Barker Bridge brewery, incorporating the magnificent Hewenden Viaduct into the logo: "I've grown up seeing this landmark every day."

Appropriately, his first beer was the delicately hopped **Arch Blonde** (4%) – and the Bay Horse at Oxenhope found a place for this on the bar in November 2022, just in time for Matt's own coming-of-age party. His second was the full-bodied, biscuity amber bitter **3 B's** (4.2%). Mosaic hops lend their ripe fruit influence to his newest beer, the session IPA **Supped Up** (3.8%).

Still only 21, and still a one-man band, Matt has already sold his cask beers into pubs from Hebden Bridge to Otley, and is looking at expanding into canning, online sales, vegan-friendly and gluten-free beers. I'm not sure even St Paul moved so fast…

Barker's Brewing

14 Midway, South Crosland, Huddersfield, HD4 7DA;
T: 07876 540211;
E: barkersbrewing@gmail.com

"I think this must be the smallest commercial brewery anywhere," says James Barker showing me around the converted stables at the top of his garden.

Teaching four days a week at a local high school, James spends Wednesdays working on his 15-gallon plant, filling around 120 cans in each batch, which are sold through a small clutch of local stores. "No-one else would do it at this scale, but it gives me a good work-life balance."

It also allowed James to rise to a personal challenge: "I was trying to make a point to myself, and discover whether I could make it in the big bad world."

Local brewers Milltown and Summer Wine helped turn James's home-brew operation into a small business, as he invested time and money during the pandemic into new equipment including a canning machine and a pump to take his waste water to the main drain. Building a small private bar in his back garden was a further lockdown project, and it was here that I first made acquaintance with the full-bodied, heady American Pale Ale **Overload** (4.6%). Deceptively sweet and gentle satsuma background belies the strength of the lovely IPA **Back for More** (6%).

"One big problem at brewing at this scale is that you still have to buy everything in bulk," says James. So he has excess hop pellets in the freezer, a big store of malt – and enough canning labels to last for years.

 **Chilly Bin** (5.6%)

In the past four years James has produced a dizzying array of brews, including the powerful American amber **Red Eye** (5.9%) and the bold, wood-smoke porter **Roger's Mistake** (5.6%). "They're both frustrating beers," he says. "The flavours you can get in dark beers is amazing, but it's really hard to sell them. Everyone seems to be looking for IPAs." Of which he makes several, including this big tasting New Zealand pale, named after Kiwi slang for a cool box. Though driven by a host of southern hemisphere hops, it's not especially bitter, but instead packed with sunshine fruit flavours – peach, mango and, perhaps appropriately, Kiwi. And given its strength, this is dangerously easy-drinking.

Bayonet Brewing

Cotswold Street, Brompton, Northallerton, DL6 2BX; w: bayonetbrewing.co.uk
e: Alex@bayonetbrewing.co.uk; 🇫 🇩 🅾 *@bayonetbrewing*

It was while judging the 2022 Flavours of Herriot Country Awards that I first made acquaintance with Bayonet, which had only been established late the previous year. Their cloudy, tropical-fruit delight **One Pip Wonder** (4.5%), packed with grapefruit, passion fruit and pineapple, was a standout performer, winning for brewer Alex Postles the first of what is sure to be a string of awards.

As a serving army officer at nearby Catterick Garrison, Alex divides his time between the barracks and the brewhouse in the garage at his home. The brewery name, the logo and the names of the beers all reflect his military connections. Named after the derisory term for a Second Lieutenant, One Pip Wonder remains his biggest seller.

The potent, multi-hopped IPA **Millionaires Weekend** (6.5%) is a homage to payday, when young squaddies hit the town and spend too much of their pay, while the super-strong double IPA **Endex** (8%) is named for the welcome command that an army training exercise is over. A new addition to the range is the easy-going pale ale **Delta Lima Six** (4%) – phonetic speak for the local postcode.

And it's within this district that Alex is determined to make a still greater

BAYONET BREWING
**DELTA LIMA SIX
TOWN PALE**
CITRA, HARLEQUIN
4%

BAYONET BREWING
**MILLIONAIRES
WEEKEND
IPA**
GALAXY, CITRA, SABRO
6.5%

BAYONET BREWING
**ONE PIP
WONDER
DDH PALE ALE**
SIMCOE
4.8%

IN COLLABORATION WITH
ROUNTON COFFEE ROASTERS
BAYONET BREWING
**THE GOOD
IDEAS CLUB**
COFFEE STOUT
7.2%
Store Cold • Drink Fresh

impact. "I'd intended to start a small brewery for a number of years but due to military commitments this wasn't ever possible," he says. "As soon as I moved to Northallerton, it soon became apparent that the town and surrounding area was the perfect place to bring this to fruition.

"The establishment of a hop-forward craft brewery in the town has created a lot of excitement and the reaction has been extremely positive since the initial launch with almost universal praise for the initial beers released.

"We are focused on community and are intent on collaborating with those around us, both small businesses and other breweries, to bring something special to the area. Our long-term goal is to bring a fully functioning brewery and taproom to the town for everyone to enjoy. This will only enhance the local economy and help to create a destination for other craft beer enthusiasts to visit."

Even so, Bayonet's fame has bagun to spread, with Alex's beers now regularly served in Stockton, Thornaby, Middlesbrough, Doncaster and Buxton. Recent orders have seen them reach bottle shops in Manchester and London, while an appearance on The Beer Fridge Podcast brought him to a national audience. Extra kit to expand capacity is helping to meet this growing demand.

The Good Ideas Club (7.2%)

Dark as night, as gnarled and comfortable as old leather, smoky, rich, meaty and dangerously strong, The Good Ideas Club is one of the very best beers I have been privileged to try during my research for this third edition of the *Yorkshire Beer Bible*. This formidable stout is the result of a collaboration with Northallerton coffee roasters Rounton, and their influence is felt in the rich, espresso-like firmness of this hedonistic swamp of sensations. It's like chewing the moist end of a Cuban cigar in an all-night bar just two streets from danger.

Baytown

*Station Road Stores, Station Road, Robin Hood's Bay, Whitby, YO22 4RA;
T: 01947 880202; W: baytownrhb.com; E: rhbaytown@gmail.com;*
🅕 *@baytownrhb;* 🅣 *@smugglergeorge*

Locals excise the outlaw from its name; to those who live here this is Baytown or simply Bay.

Search online for the story of the brewery and you'll find tales of contraband, hidden tunnels and secret recipes – and the ancient diary of a smuggler revealing scrapes with the customs men. The website makes great play of the fact that the village's dramatic location in the cliffs may once have been the setting for this most ancient of criminal professions. The story it doesn't reveal is that, rather than being brewed here, the beers are actually smuggled across from some way inland, Hambleton Brewery having taken over where the now-closed Cropton left off.

But there's some quality ale behind the hype. Pale and malty **Press Gang's Arrival** (4.2%) is an entry-level easy-drinking refreshing ale while the full-bodied **Smuggler's Haul** (6%) concentrates these flavours into a simple, bold, strong bitter. **Squire's Connivance** (5%) is a dark porter packed with chocolate, liquorice and aniseed, **Revenue's Revenge** (4.2%) a crisp, sharp lager.

Baytown Bitter (4%) pours an attractive pale golden brown, topped with an extravagant foaming head. While there's no significant aroma, once on the palate it charges around like a cutlass-wielding pirate, showing off a sweetish full-bodied malty weight. Only in the finish does the balance tip towards the bitterness of the hops, just as it should in a traditional, sessionable Yorkshire bitter.

Beer Ink

Plover Road Garage, Plover Road, Lindley, Huddersfield, HD3 3PJ;
T: 01484 643368; W: beer-ink.co.uk; E: Sales@beer-ink.co.uk;
🅵 *@BeerInk.ltd;* 🐦 *@BeerInkBrewCo;* 📷 *@beer.ink*

Ryan Stoppard, right, and Gavin Kieran manning the Beer Ink bar at Sheffield Indie Beer Feast

This former garage site was first taken on as a brewery by Mallinsons in 2008, and also hosted the now-defunct Hand Drawn Monkey, before Beer Ink began production here in 2016 – since when brewer Ryan Stoppard has created a host of different brews, some mainstream, others more experimental. They are enjoyed in the on-site taproom and quality alehouses nearby.

Since the last edition of the *Yorkshire Beer Bible* in 2019, Ryan has shaken up his range and now offers a core roster of five – including the juicy New England pale **Typo** (4%), beautiful blackberry-accented stout **Lampblack** (4.6%), tropical fruit IPA **Scrawler** (5%) and crisp, slightly lemony lager **Gutenberg** (4.2%).

"I do like to experiment," Ryan tells me over a beer at Sheffield Indie Beer Feast in March 2023. He hands over a glass of the impressive, luxurious coffee and chocolate **Red Eye / Hidden Gold** (5.6%), itself a cask ale blend of the cacao-enriched **Hidden Gold** (5%) and the espresso stout **Red Eye** (6%), brewed with 30 litres of espresso and grounds from local roastery Frazer's. "I like to go down the road of beers which no-one else is doing," he adds. These have included the rhubarb sour **Stalk of Life** (4%) and the fascinating, baffling, left-field **Bloody Mary Gose** (5.2%), which emerged from a partnership with Kyiv brewer Didko.

In the sociable world of modern brewing, Ryan has further indulged his passion for great new beer through collaborations with some of the cream of Yorkshire's brewing scene – Wilde Child, Ridgeside, Lost Industry and Abbeydale among them.

Vellum (4%)

In keeping with the brewery's name, several of the beers follow the same printing theme. Since Roman times, Vellum has been derived from animal skin, and is still used for writing or occasionally printing, usually for documents of major importance. It's perhaps surprising that this high-end product should lend its name to an entry-level pale ale, but a curiosity explained by the fact that Vellum offers more in style, substance and character than many storied ales far stronger. A heavy dose of American Citra and Amarillo hops lend their weight to this cloudy golden brew, which simmers with citric promise on the nose and then bursts onto the palate with more mango and grapefruit than a tropical fruit salad. Remarkable.

Beespoke Brewery

The Fox, 41 Briggate, Shipley, BD17 7BP; T: 01274 594826;
W: thefoxshipley.co.uk; @beespokebrewery

"It doesn't really look like this on Google Maps."

We're only minutes into a Saturday afternoon pub crawl of Shipley and Saltaire and self-appointed navigator Diane is already staring at her phone, looking confused. "It's supposed to be a big place set back from the road," she says, with an air somewhere between puzzlement and indignation, as we file into the Fox, an excellent micropub just outside the centre of Shipley.

The pub was established by Chris Bee, co-founder of the former Salamander brewery – and the addition of a one-barrel brewing plant in the cellars brought a new dimension to a venue which prides itself on running a year-round beer festival, with an ever-changing selection of six cask ales on draft.

These will usually include at least one from Beespoke. For me, the standout ale is the sleepy, silky, delicate **Shipley Stout** (4.6%), while others include the firm and bitter **Beeboppalula** (4.2%) and the full-bodied, sweet and malty **Clocktower Porter** (5.5%).

Anyway, back on our pub crawl, it is at least three hours later, when we're in the beer garden of the Boathouse at Saltaire enjoying the fourth or fifth pint of a very convivial afternoon, when Diane finally admits that she'd actually been looking at a map of Shipley in the West Midlands...

Belschnickel Brewery *New*

*146 Ella Street, Hull, HU5 3AU; T: 01482 348747; W: www.belschnickel.co.uk;
E: kevin@belschnickel.co.uk; ☐ @belschnickelbrewery;
☐ @belschnickel_brewery; ☐ @belsch_brewery*

At some breweries, the back story is almost as interesting as the beers. Stuttgart-born Kevin Berthold spent ten years in the German airforce before moving to Berlin to study film directing. Here he met Bridlington-born Rachel, a biological anthropologist whose speciality is the nocturnal lemurs of Madagascar.

The couple first dreamed of opening a brewery while living in Germany, and later began home-brewing after moving to Glasgow. The strictures of lockdown – and the opportunity of converting a garden outbuilding at their new home in Hull – finally allowed this dream to become reality.

"We're not trying to reinvent the wheel," says Kevin. "We just want to do justice to the history, traditions, culture and flavours of our beers by letting the malts, hops and yeast do the talking. We use our labelling to try to tell a little of these stories, and their personal connection to us."

Their first beer release, the traditional Gose **Pfaffendorf** (4.1%) is a good example. It's named after Kevin's great-grandfather who was Mayor of Goslar, where this distinctive sour and salty beer style originated; his portrait on the can hangs in the home of Kevin's grandmother. A gold award in SIBA's national beer contest in 2023 was an early success for this sharp, yeasty, sour white wine brew. Smooth, espresso martini-like Irish extra stout **Schwarzer Kater** (6.8%) is another core beer, while there is a clovey suggestion of a wheat beer to the light and refreshing, slightly sour table saison **Erntechelfer** (4.9%).

With a maximum brew of 90 litres for cans and 35 litres for bottles, Kevin and Rachel make a virtue of their nano-brewery size: "It enables us to try a range of different beer styles on a small scale and get our beers out and drunk whilst fresh and at their best. We do everything in-house between the two of us, allowing us to keep a close eye on quality control."

Sold in 75cl champagne bottles, corked and capped, Belschnickel's Avenues Collection celebrates the distinctive architecture of Hull's Avenues area, where the brewery is based. These include the saison **Ella** (6.4%), Imperial Stout **Victoria** (9.3%), Belgian pale ale **Westbourne** (6%) and the Belgian strong dark ale **Marlborough** (11.5%).

🍺 Hullywood (3.9%)
A light haze clouds this generously-portioned amber IPA, "a celebration of Hull and hops" according to the label. While there is some modest yeast character to the aroma, it bursts onto the palate with a faintly sour and earthy blend of tangerine and stewed apples, and departs with a prolonged dryness on the back of the throat. It packs plenty of punch for ale of such sessionable strength.

Bingley Brewery

2, Old Mill Yard, Shay Lane, Wilsden, Bradford, BD15 0DR; T: 01535 274285;
W: bingleybrewery.co.uk; E: info@bingleybrewery.co.uk;
�facebook *@bingleybrewery.co.uk;* 🐦 📷 *@BingleyBrewery*

Owner and brewer Darren Marks established Bingley Brewery in 2014 and has built a strong local reputation around products such as toffee and citrus blonde ale **Goldy Locks** (4%), roasted malt and liquorice stout **1848** (4.8%) and spicy, berry-bearing red ale **Blantyre** (5%). Drinkers who love their hop-front American-influenced pales will find the juicy, piny, slightly spicy **Jamestown** (5.4%) well worth a visit.

Their on-site brewery bar does a healthy trade, opening on the first Friday of the month and occasional Saturdays, when Bingley beers can pair nicely with the fare from local street food providers.

Bini Brew Co *New*

Unit A, Wharfe View Rd, Ilkley, LS29 8DU; T: 01943 514361;
W: binibrew.co; E: hello@binibrew.co; 🎵 🐦 📷 *@BiniBrew*

James Rudge and Richard Thackray met while working at Leeds beer and charcuterie venue Friends of Ham; furlough during the pandemic gave them the opportunity to turn James's home-brewing operation into a business. "I was a complete novice," admits Richard. "I've been selling beer for years, but brewing it is a different kettle of fish. I am learning all the time."

By July 2021 they had moved into business premises in Ilkley, establishing a three-barrel kit which turns out some characteristically juicy and hazy pale ales such as their flagship dry and bitter ale **Under the Manhole Cover** (4.3%) which is fermented with New England yeast and was perfected over long evenings of lockdown. **Cedric the Seagull** is a 4.5% cherry gose, while IPA **Breaking Dad** (6.5%) presumably honours James's father Nick, a third partner in the enterprise.

These and more have already found favour with drinkers in the Market Town Taverns pubs, their alma mater Friends of Ham, and further afield.

Unlike businesses whose plans and projections were utterly destroyed by Covid, breweries that began life during the pandemic always knew the conditions they would be facing. "We didn't have bills to pay, we weren't relying on big orders, we weren't carrying any debt," says James. "And at the start we were working full time."

James Rudge and Richard Thackray serving customers at
Leeds International Beer Festival in September 2022

🍺 Chairman Miaow (5.5%)

Named to honour the brewery cat Bini – itself
named after their favourite holiday place,
Binibeca in Menorca – this is a classic
New England IPA. Both aroma and taste
are packed with tropical fruit, the product
of Citra and Mosaic hops in the brew,
and some significant dry hopping with
Citra and El Dorado. It's emblematic of a
young ambitious brewery on the rise.

Black Sheep Brewery

Wellgarth, Crosshills, Masham, HG4 4EN; T: 01765 689227;
W: blacksheepbrewery.com; E: reception@blacksheep.co.uk;
🅕 🅞 *@blacksheepbrewery;* 🅣 *@blacksheepbeer*

One of the unforeseen consequences of the war in Ukraine is that it robbed Yorkshire of one of its most remarkable beers. I've written several times about the complex sensory smorgasbord of Black Sheep's

wonderful **Imperial Russian Stout** (8.5%) – aromas of red wine and decadent, narcotic Turkish coffee giving way to black treacle and caramel on the palate, all resolving into a smoky finish, pricked with the tartness of blackcurrant. At a time when few would wish to celebrate Russian imperialism, Putin's invasion saw the brewery remove the beer from its roster, and it has yet to return.

The story of how separate branches of the Theakston family came to own Masham's two rival brewers has been so oft-told it hardly bears further repetition. Both trace a bloodline to Robert Theakston, who turned his back on the family's cattle farm to lease the town's Black Bull brewhouse in 1827. Theakston's retain his name, Black Sheep prize their 'first son' provenance.

Townsfolk tend to take sides. Most have a connection to one or other brewery, and choose their pint accordingly. "Masham folk tend to drink either Theakston Best or Black Sheep Bitter," one local tells me. The stronger beers – Old Peculier and Riggwelter – are "mostly for the tourists."

Of which there are plenty. Around 50,000 call in at the Black Sheep visitor centre every year, many joining the hour-long tour which winds through the site before ending at the attractive Bistro and Baaa'r (geddit), where a proud line of handpumps dispenses their famous core cask ales: dry, peppery, sessionable **Best Bitter** (3.8%), full bodied **Black Sheep Special Ale** (4.4%) and big-tasting fruit-cakey **Riggwelter** (5.9%).

To that range has recently been added gently citric IPA **Respire** (4%), their first carbon-neutral cask beer, launched on Earth Day 2022 with

a contribution from each sale supporting tree planting in the Dales. Each is brewed in traditional Yorkshire Square vessels – they are stainless steel and circular these days, but the process is precisely the same as when they were four-cornered and made of slate.

A restless spirit for experimentation

Blossom is a brand-new beer conceptualised, brewed and branded by the women in the Black Sheep team, to mark International Women's Day.

has seen a host of new beers added to the roster in recent times, not least two milkshake IPAs, one flavoured with mango and another with raspberry and white chocolate. Both were winners at the 2021 World Beer Awards, as were the **Milk Stout** (4.4%) and its more powerful crazy cousins **Peanut Brittle Stout** (6.9%) and **Hazelnut and Salted Caramel Stout** (7.2%). The lovely jet-black **Choc Orange Stout** (6.1%) brings to the palate the complexity of cigar smoke, black coffee, chilli and lime, to add to the Terry's Chocolate Orange of the aroma.

Black Sheep Brewery is one of British brewing's most famous stories and has grown from humble beginnings to become a multi-award-winning company, with its beers enjoyed around the world. More than 30 years on, founder Paul Theakston remains company chairman, though the day-to-day running of the brewery has long since passed to sons Rob and Jo. As we went to press, the shock news broke that Black Sheep had been placed into administration. One hopes that this is but a temporary measure, and that the brewery and its pubs can survive.

🍺 **Holy Grail** (4.7%)

Black Sheep are rightly proud of their long-standing tie-up to the Monty Python crew – and created this beer in 1999 to celebrate 30 years of their ground-breaking comedy. Tempered over burning witches and with more bite than a killer rabbit, this bright golden ale has a tight creamy head and a lovely zesty nose, and packs in bags of refreshing citric flavour, leading into a long dry finish. The perfect foil for a meal of spam, spam, eggs, beans and spam, it's great for drinking beside your shrubbery.

Blue Bee Brewery

Unit 29-30, Hoyland Road Industrial Estate, Sheffield, S3 8AB;
T: 07375 659349; W: bluebeebrewery.co.uk; E: sales@bluebeebrewery.co.uk;
f **y** *@bluebeebrewery*

The pandemic coincided with the tenth anniversary of Blue Bee and caused two long interruptions to brewing. This was doubtless a serious inconvenience to drinkers at the famous Kelham Island Tavern – Sheffield CAMRA's 2020 pub of the year – which has long offered this cask-only brewery a ready route to market. Full production finally got back under way in 2021.

Hefty, flag-waving quantities of mosaic, citra and equinox hops created the patriotic bugle blast of citrus and tropical fruit in Blue Bee's **Born in the USA** (6%) which was Champion at Huddersfield Beer Festival in 2016. Now just an occasional, this wonderful example of a new age IPA complements the brewery's regular range which includes summery, floral **Reet Pale** (4%) and traditional bronze-coloured bitter **Hillfoot Best** (4%). Full-bodied **Export Stout** (6.6%) derives roasted coffee and chocolate flavours from the seven different malt breweries in the brew.

Smooth roasted **Damflask Dark Mild** (3.8%) made a first appearance at CAMRA's members' weekend in April 2023.

This ten-barrel cask-only brewery's relentlessly adventurous spirit spawns an ever-changing list of specials, seasonals, collaborations and occasionals.

Bone Idle Brewing Company

The White Swan, 28 The Green, Idle, Bradford, BD10 9PX; T: 07525 751574;
E: jimemmett@btinternet.com; 🅵 @boneidlebrewery

Like the world-famous Idle Working Men's
Club, this brewery makes good use of its
curious location. The brewery was founded
in a converted barn not long before Covid-19
arrived. All its beers are sold through the Idle
Draper pub next door, which is worth a visit if
ever you have an Idle moment.

Bone Machine

Taphouse Brewpub, 70 Humber St, Hull, HU1 1TU; T: 01482 618000; W: bone-machine-brew-co.myshopify.com; E: beer@bonemachinebrewing.com; @bonemachinebrewco; @bonemachinebrew

Close to Hull's historic waterfront, in former fruit market warehouses rediscovered by the city's burgeoning Arts Quarter, the Taphouse venue is right at the heart of an £80m regeneration. Taphouse is East Yorkshire's largest brewpub and combines a brewery with a high-quality bar offering almost 40 draught craft beers, lagers and ciders, as well as an extensive range of bottled and canned beers. Drinkers can watch the brewers at work in the rear of the bar, while regular tours allow them to get up close and personal with the process.

When it launched it 2019, it became a new waterfront home for Finnish brothers Marko and Kimi Karjalainen who had established Bone Machine in Pocklington two years earlier and now distribute their distinctive brews across the UK and to outlets in Finland, Sweden and the Netherlands.

Their range, which stretches from the fiercely traditional to the experimental and contemporary, changes all the time: "We try to make anything and everything," says Marko. "We make beers that we like to drink, but we like to experiment with different grains, such as rice and sorghum." They have a penchant for a collab, too.

I've caught up with a few. Hazy yellow **Garden Of Death** (7%) is an in-your-face New England IPA with a blast of musty fruit zests in the aroma and a taste dominated by pineapple, with a counter-intuitively pleasant undercurrent of stewing vegetables.

The powerful stout **Mary Ann Is Dead** (7.4%) has the chocolate notes you often find with these strong dark roasty ales – but here the brothers blend it with mint to create an engaging flavour often explored in ice cream and after-dinner sweets, but rarely in beer. Several others in the range reference mortality in the name, but not all.

"It has been very difficult during the pandemic," says Marko. "But we are still trading, still brewing the beers we love and still having a bit of fun."

🍺 Mastiff (10.5%)

This purebred beauty was one of the 'best in show' contenders at the Leeds International Beer Festival in September 2022. Named to honour one of Hull's hardest, heaviest rock bands, this creamy imperial stout is given extra weight and substance by coffee grains from local roasters the Blending Room. Its jet-black colour and dark brooding nature echo the serious Goth leanings of a brewery which clearly likes to push flavour sensations to the limit.

BONE MACHINE BREW CO
x
MAS†IFF
imperial coffee stout
10.5% alc. vol.

Bosun's Brewery

15 Sandbeck Park, Wetherby, LS22 7TW; T: 01937 227337;
W: bosunsbrewery.com; E: hello@bosunsbrewery.com; 🇫 🇩 *@bosunsbrewery*

Like some storm-tossed sailing ship, Bosun's has seen its share of adventures before finding a safe haven in Wetherby.

It was first established over ten years ago in Horbury, the name reflecting brewer Grahame Andrews' previous career at sea. And there it stayed for several years, before flooding – and the opportunity to expand into larger premises – saw Bosun's sail west to Huddersfield, where Grahame hoisted the brewery flag over its first on-site bar.

In February 2020, just as the pandemic began to take hold, it was bought by a group of friends who had run East Keswick's beer festival for several years. "Good fortune and hard work saw us through lockdown," says new co-owner James McGregor-Tosh, who then oversaw the ten-barrel brewery's latest voyage, 40 miles north-west to Wetherby.

We're talking in the convivial taproom alongside the brewery. Here groups of friends and families are enjoying the great beers brewed next door, while their children are playing table football and video games. The pizza vendor in the corner is doing a roaring trade.

"It has really taken off, and that gives us real confidence for the future," says James. Even so, he and his partners have retained their day jobs: "We're not at a stage where we can rely on this to pay the mortgage and feed our families."

The brewing is handled by Garry Preece and Rowena Esp, who made the move across with the brewery from Huddersfield: "We're very lucky, because they know the business really well," says James. Some of their beers retain the nautical names from Bosun's early

days. The no-nonsense earthy, full-bodied brown ale **Maiden Voyage** (3.9%) was the first to be released and I have a real soft spot for the sharper, full-bodied, bright and golden IPA **King Neptune** (4.4%). Others include **Blonde** (3.9%) whose yeasty, bready aroma and malty, wheaty nature are sharpened by some strident juicy fruit hop character in the later throes of the taste.

These modest strengths exemplify a determination to stick largely to traditional brews, though a pilot kit in the brewery does allow Garry and Rowena to experiment, and try out potential new recipes on the taproom customers. "But we're not going to do anything too crackers," James insists.

Some of the output goes to bottling and canning – but the brewery's cask and keg ales now enjoy a wide distribution, both to freehouses and to the Stonegate chain. Given the name, it's perhaps no surprise that pubs on the east coast, in Whitby, Filey and Bridlington, are among their most regular customers.

 Best (4%)

A hand-pulled pint of this fiercely traditional Yorkshire bitter provides the gentle accompaniment to my chat with James at the Wetherby taproom. It certainly looks the part – a lovely translucent copper colour – and malt dominates the taste, distributing soft biscuity flavours across the palate. Any bitter character is modest and understated in this perfect session ale which should appeal to mariner and landlubber alike.

Both Barrels Brewing

56a Main Street, Mexborough; T: 07753 746618;
E: anthony@bothbarrelsbrewing.com; **f** *@both_barrels_brewing*

This newbie, established during the pandemic is focused on small batches of unfiltered, unpasteurised ales and lagers. After a hiatus during 2022, Both Barrels roared back in March 2023 with the sizeable liquorice and coffee **Patriot** stout (4.2%).

Bradfield Brewery

Watt House Farm, High Bradfield, Sheffield, S36 1BT; T: 0114 2851118;
W: bradfieldbrewery.com; E: info@bradfieldbrewery.com;
🅵 *@bradfieldbrewery;* 🆇 *@BradfieldBrew*

September 2020 marked a milestone at Bradfield – and to honour their 5,000th brew, brewers Sam, Bruce and Kieran used five different hops and five different malts during a 24-hour brewathon to create their new IPA **5K** (5%). It was emblematic of a brewery determined to ride out the pandemic, pivoting their operation from on-sales to local home deliveries. In 2021 they released a series of limited edition **Kerry Imperial Stouts** (7.5%-8%), some aged in spirit barrels and sold in 75cl bottles. They quickly sold out.

Watt House was a working Peak District dairy farm before its diversification into brewing; they went from milking 100 cows a week to brewing 100,000 pints of ale a week, using pure millstone grit springwater. The first pint was served in 2005 at The Nags Head in Loxley; this and the King and Miller in Deepcar are now the two brewery taps. Their award-winning ultra-pale **Blonde** (4%) with its marked citrus and summer fruit aromas is their entry-level product, with other permanents including oat-fortified **Stout** (4.5%), and big-selling winter ale, **Belgian Blue** (4.9%), while a good list of seasonals completes the catalogue. The brewery is a big sponsor of Sheffield ice-hockey side the Steeldogs.

🍺 Bradfield Farmer's Pale Ale (5%)
Some fresh, floral notes emerge from the foaming white head of the aroma of this dry and fruity beer. On the palate its quiet toffee flavours are neatly balanced by some determined hoppy bitterness, the tastes zipped around by some zingy, prickly carbonation.

Brass Castle Brewery

10A Yorkersgate, Malton, YO17 7AB; T: 01653 698683;
W: brasscastle.co.uk; E: online@brasscastlebrewery.co.uk;
🅕 *@brasscastlebrewery;* 🅧 🅞 *@brasscastlebeer*

Though the brewery has long since relocated from Phil Saltonstall's one-barrel plant in his garage, Pocklington's Brass Castle Hill is immortalised by his quality craft beers which have gained an enthusiastic following both in Yorkshire and overseas. From those humble beginnings, Phil's team now produces a great range of gluten-free, vegan and vegetarian-friendly beers: imperial stouts, weizenbocks, sours, triple IPAs, witbiers, fruit beers and more. Animal-derived products aren't allowed near the Brass Castle brewhouse, and this commitment to ecology extends to spent hops enriching the produce of local allotments and spent grain being used to create biogas and fertiliser.

Vanilla porter **Bad Kitty** (5.5%), the second beer he ever brewed, remains Brass Castle's best-known product. It's available in many formats, including wood barrel-aged, rum and Christmas-spiced variants, as well as a new nitro-keg version.

The core range includes malt-forward classic **Northern Blonde** (3.9%), lemon and floral-accented **Pilsen Thrills** (3.9%) and hop-swap beer **Misfit** (4.3%) which features regularly-changing hop combinations. **Sunshine** (5.7%) celebrates the classic IPA style while **Disruptor** (7.4%) is a temperate juicy rendition of the modern New England-style IPA. A cider brewed with ale yeast and apple juice is set to join the range soon.

Hoptical Illusion (4.3%) is the gluten-free version of their single hopped **Comet** (4.3%) pale ale. It pours a dull, slightly cloudy pale gold, and has a beautiful rich, dry, bitterness to the taste, no doubt the product of the hops, but not overly fruity or piney – and with absolutely bags of taste for a beer of its moderate strength. It even delivers a little warming glow in the finish.

The Brewery Taphouse in the centre of Malton is open Tuesday through Sunday and offers cosy comfort amid reclaimed wood and barrels; a crowler machine allows drinkers to take away just under a litre of their favourite beer in a sealed can filled at the bar. Quiz nights, vinyl sessions and occasional tap takeovers freshen up the local night scene.

Meet Me Underwater (6.5%)
With its beautiful label by Yorkshire artist Malcolm Ludvigsen, this one practically leapt off the shelf when I called in on the wonderful Ossett bottle shop Bier Huis recently. Its suggestion of salt is derived from seaweed harvested in the North Sea and thrown into this complex red ale of barley wine strength. Thankfully those savoury notes don't overpower the cakey, bready, almost chewy tastes of this wonderful vegan gluten-free night cap.

BrewSocial *New*

Princess Street, Sheffield, S4 7UU

There's a strong community ethos – and some striking scarlet casks – to this new Sheffield brewery, whose home is a railway arch in Attercliffe, north-west of the city centre.

As an alumnus of Abbeydale, Acorn, Blue Bee and more, I can only imagine that brewer Richard Hough specialises in the early letters of the alphabet. Here he has placed an emphasis on providing employment for those disadvantaged in the labour market, and is working with local social development agency Y2V to provide opportunities in brewing, cleaning, delivery, marketing and more.

The nine-barrel kit has seen previous service with at least two other brewers, most recently Sheffield's Little Ale Cart, and recent brews include the hazy pale **'lypso** (4.6%) and the blonde **Jester Minute** (3.7%). The copper-coloured chestnutty bitter **Crackin' Nuts** (4%) made a welcome appearance at CAMRA's members' weekend in April 2023.

Brew York

Unit 6, Enterprise Complex, Walmgate, York, YO1 9TT; T: 01904 848448;
W: brewyork.co.uk; E: admin@brewyork.co.uk; 🄵 🄳 🄾 *@brewyorkbeer*

Wayne Smith and Lee Grabham first met at the stag weekend of a mutual friend, and soon channelled their shared passion for craft beer into a home-brewing operation which rapidly turned into something still more remarkable.

Brew York burst spectacularly onto the local scene in 2016, shrugging off the significant setback of metre-deep flooding to their riverside premises just weeks after Wayne and Lee had signed the lease.

Their relentless passion for innovation is reflected in an eclectic brew range which usually runs to at least 20 fresh beers at any one time. "Our approach to brewing has always been to produce the types of beers which we would love to drink in can, keg and cask," says marketing manager Pete English.

"Our beers are inspired by many different things: the rich and diverse surroundings of Yorkshire; a new hop or ingredient we want to try; a cocktail or dessert we want to translate into a beer. We love to experiment with ingredients and styles and we find inspiration in pop culture, films and music which we combine with a desire to create full-flavour and impactful brews.

"We may well be well-known for our quirky and playful approach to brewing, but everything we do is done with passion and attention to detail."

Collaborations, limited releases and varying iterations of the core range keep things interesting. Their expansion to a new £2m production facility east of the city centre at Osbaldwick with its own taproom – and further venues in Pocklington and Leeds – are confident signs of Brew York's continuing success.

With its luscious, lustrous, sweet black darkness, the coconut, tonka bean, vanilla and cacao milk stout **Tonkoko** (4.3%) earned the brewery

some early fame, with first prize at the city's beer festival. Others in the core range include the juice-bucket pale ale **Calmer Chameleon** (3.8%), crisp Czech-inspired lager **Golden Eagle** (4.8%) and fruity IPA **Juice Forsyth** (5%).

There's plenty of lovely hop bitterness to the golden West Coast pale **Brave Noise** (5.2%) whose juicy, lemony zing is given extra urgency by some determined carbonation.

Back at the mothership in Walmgate, the brewery sits alongside a taproom where you can watch the brewers at work and enjoy the beer right beside the tanks which gave them life. A stunning beer garden looks out across the water to the impressive Rowntree Wharf; flood protection measures now guard against any future swelling of the Foss.

 Coffee (10%)

In my early days of beer writing, I'm not sure I could ever have been convinced that a brewery would one day market a maple mocha iced latte stout. Thankfully, the world has moved on, brewers have evolved into creatures of endless creativity; drinkers have been educated to expect and demand new flavours and experiences. This one is lovely – jet-black, packed with coffee of a gently soothing nature and softer on the palate than the bitter kick of an espresso. The maple lends a touch of sweetness to a beer which never quite feels as strong as its double digit percentage would imply.

Bricknell Brewery

Bricknell Avenue, Hull, HU5 4ET; W: bricknellbrewery.co.uk;
E: Richard@bricknellbrewery.co.uk; 🐦 *@BricknellBeers;* 📷 *@BricknellBrewery*

Tiny Bricknell is the very essence of a one-man band. It was established
by former Hull University lecturer Richard English who sold his sports car
to set up the brewery in his garage in 2015 – and he does everything
himself, from the brewing and bottling to the label sticking and delivery.

With a typical brew length of just 160 litres, Richard specialises in the
production of unusual hand-crafted bottle-conditioned beers for just a
handful of local bars and restaurants, though an occasional cask makes
its way into the on-trade and to local beer festivals.

His range starts with straw-coloured **Saazy Blonde** (4%) a crisp and
fresh-tasting real ale targeted at the lager drinkers. **Cascade Pale** (4.4%)
is an American-style pale ale, brewed with lashings of Cascade hops
which exert an energetic grapefruit influence on the aroma and flavour.
Richard's stronger ales include the luxuriously treacly Imperial Russian
Stout **Slavanka 1873** (7%), named after a ship built in Hull for the
Russian Tsars.

Limitations of space have persuaded him to reduce his range in recent years, notably by slashing his railway-themed flavoured porters from the roster, and simply replacing them with the traditional **Wilberforce Porter** (4.9%). "Keeping them all in stock requires a large storeroom which has to be air-conditioned for several months each year. The cost of this is huge, so I want to reduce the range and use a smaller storeroom that hopefully won't cost as much to keep cool in the summer."

But without the considerable overheads which burden some other brewers of similar size, this remains a profitable trade: "I really do it because I love it," says Richard. "It's just an extension of my hobby."

🍺 **Bosphorous 1875** (6%)

This has long been one of my favourites from the Bricknell range, and is a beer which has proved popular with guests at my regular beer tasting events. It's a traditional mild, based on a Victorian recipe from the days when this style was chiefly a working man's refresher, synonymous with low alcohol and a lack of flavour. Instead, this is a slightly sweet, dark ruby ale, not noticeably bitter, but with a rich, malty, slightly sweet flavour – and sufficient warmth and depth to remind you of its premium strength.

Bridgehouse Brewery

Airedale Heifer, Bradford Road, Sandbeds, Keighley, BD20 5LY;
T: 01535 601222; W: bridgehousebrewery.co.uk;
E: info@bridgehousebrewery.co.uk; 🔵 📷 *@bridgehousebrewery;*
🔵 *@BBrewery*

The popular Craven Heifer is the fourth location for a brewery which began life in Keighley in 2010 using kit salvaged from Sowerby Bridge's defunct Ryburn Brewery.

They soon moved to Oxenhope, before merging with the brewery at the Old White Bear pub in Keighley. A purpose-built 15-barrel plant at the popular foody pub in Sandbeds has at last found Bridgehouse a permanent home. From here they also service a chain of 12 pubs.

The brewery neatly namechecks the region of its wanderings with the flagship pale amber **Aired Ale** (4.1%), whose citric, slightly floral aroma gives way to juicy, biscuity flavours on the palate, with just a hint of spice, and a lingering, dry finish. There's a real zip to the zingy **Tequila Blonde** (3.8%) while golden **Holy Cow** (5.6%) bursts with theatrical levels of juicy, fruity hop flavour.

Bridgehouse Porter (4.5%)

During a recent visit to Haworth, I discovered that each of the Brontë siblings is now honoured with a Bridgehouse Brew – the biscuity pale amber **Emily** (4.1%), the easy-going gently bitter blonde **Anne** (4%), the slightly sweet IPA **Charlotte** (5.6%) and the appropriately darker **Branwell** (4.5%). The Black Bull, at the top of the village's cobbled main street celebrates its connections with Branwell, the wayward artist brother of the three authors, who was a frequent customer here. And it was here that I made acquaintance with this wonderful deep ruby porter, full-bodied and impossibly smooth, topped with a firm yet creamy head, which bathes the palate in soothing, balming, warming malt, liquorice and toffee.

Bridlington Brewing

The Pack Horse, Market Place, Bridlington, YO16 4QJ; T: 01262 674592

Local real ale favourite the Pack Horse is the ideal place to try beers from this microbrewery, which was established in the nearby Telegraph Inn's beer garden in 2014 and moved to the Pack Horse in 2017. A flurry of appropriately equine-themed beers included **Wonky Donkey** (4%), **Copper Horse** (4%) and **Farrier's Choice** (4%).

Briggs Signature Ales

Unit 1, Waterhouse Mill, 65-71 Lockwood Road, Huddersfield, HD1 3QU;
T: 07427 668004; W: briggssignatureales.weebly.com;
E: info@briggsales.co.uk; 🅵 *@briggs ales;* 🐦 *@briggssigales*

Carpenter Nick Briggs developed a love of real ale while working in the building trade. After a spell working for Mallinsons, Nick struck out on his own, producing his own music-themed ales on the Huddersfield plant. They include piney, red-berry flavoured bitter **Techno** (4.2%), the American-hop influenced **Northern Soul** (5.7%) and tropical fruit golden ale **Hip Hop** (4.2%). There's a lovely rich head to the high-octane dark fruit porter **Heavy Metal** (5.7%), while **Mash Up** (3.9%) typifies Yorkshire's "make do and mend" spirit by using hops left over from previous brews.

Talented artist Martin Simpson provides Nick with the grotesques and ne'er-do-wells who feature on the pump clips.

Briscoe's

Ash Grove, Otley, LS21 3EL; T: 01943 466515; E: briscoe.brewery@talktalk.net

Microbiologist-turned-microbrewer Paul Briscoe has been brewing cask ales for almost 40 years, initially as a home-brewer and now as a commercial brewer on a one-barrel kit in his home cellar. His brews are now less regular than they were, but can still occasionally be found in pubs nearby.

Captain Cook Brewery

White Swan, 1 West End, Stokesley, TS9 5BL; T: 01642 710263

Named after the famed local explorer, this four-barrel brewery in the northern reaches of the county was established in 1999 in the 18th-century White Swan pub, which remains the best place to sample the wares – though their cask and bottled beers are sometimes more widely available. Dark and warming **Endeavour** (4.3%) is their appropriately named flagship bitter.

Chevin Brew Co

1, Mount Pisgah, Otley, LS21 3DX; T: 07894 869082; W: chevinbrew.co;
E: chevinotley@gmail.com; 🅕 🅨 🅞 *@chevinbrewco*

Small batches of keg, cask and bottled beers are the stock-in-trade of this new microbrewer proud of its Otley heritage – using local ingredients in its beers, and the work of local artists on its labels. They share the one-barrel kit with the Marlowe Brew Project.

Beers include the milk chocolate porter **Made of Stone** (4.5%) and premium pale ale **Pale Green Man** (5.3%) while powerful IPA **Norwegian Blue** (7.5%) ramps up the ante rather further. The only one I've caught up with so far is their very light and easy-going pale ale, the fresh-tasting **Homegrown Heroes** (4.4%), brewed as part of a community hop-growing project.

Chantry Brewery

Units 1-2 Callum Court, Gateway Industrial Park, Parkgate,
Rotherham, S62 6NR; T: 01709 711866; W: chantrybrewery.co.uk;
🅕 *@chantrybreweryrotherham;* 🅧 🅞 *@chantrybrewery*

Chantry Brewery is the only brewery remaining in a town whose brewing history stretches back through companies like Bentley's and Mappin's who competed for custom among those who laboured in Rotherham's furnaces and glass factories. Fittingly, Sheffield steel was used to create this 20-barrel plant, from whence comes the fresh, light **Steelos** (4.1%) with its subtle aromas of sweet orange, apricots and blackcurrants; well-balanced pine and blackberry **Full Moon** (4.2%) and the full-bodied stout **Diamond Black** (4.5%). Oily, toasty, **Special Reserve** (6.3%) is an old ale packed with black treacle, raisins and suggestions of red wine.

Bright, crisp and refreshing **New York Pale** (3.9%) honours a local factory which once furnished the Big Apple with its distinctive red fire hydrants, and was crowned Champion Bitter of Yorkshire at the 2018 Rotherham Real Ale Music Festival, where the firm porter **Two Magpies** (4.5%) was named best porter.

The brewery has recently added an on-site bar to a portfolio which also includes the ancient Chantry Inn in Sheffield and Rotherham's New York Tavern. The famous old Cutlers Arms, a short walk from the football stadium, is an appropriately-named venue to try the whole Chantry range.

🍺 **Iron and Steel** (4%)
With this name, this simple, sessionable copper-coloured bitter could only have been forged in the industrial heartland of South Yorkshire. Several breweries which have emerged in and around Sheffield in recent years celebrate this proud heritage, with beers such as Stancill's Stainless and Toolmakers' Lynchpin. Though Iron and Steel is only brewed to a modest strength, it is possessed of sufficient toffee character and an iron-like firmness to be suggestive of something rather stronger.

Chin Chin Brewing

Unit 53F, Langthwaite Business Park, South Kirkby, Pontefract, WF9 3NS;
T: 07896 253650; E: david@chinchinbrewing.co.uk;
🅕 *@chinchinbrewing;* 🅧 *@chinchinbrewing*

The malty, sessionable amber ale **Little Boy Lost** (4.6%) is the only beer
I've so far tracked down from this newcomer, though the Soldiers in
South Elmsall and Fat Cat in Sheffield are among pubs which often sell
their wares. **Everybody's Fool** (3.9%) marked the local rhubarb festival in
February 2023 and imminent plans to start bottling should hopefully make
Chin Chin more widely available.

Cobbydale Brewery

47 Kirkgate, Silsden, BD20 0AQ; T: 07965 569885; E: lreids@gmail.com

The Cobbydale brewhouse is in the rear of the Red Lion pub in Silsden,
which remains the best place to try the beers. They include firm and fruity
Eye Pee Aye (6.1%), creamy stout **Dark Stuff** (5%) and their original
premium bitter **Cobbyd Ale** (4.8%).

Cooper Hill Brewery

Unit 4, Highcliffe Mills, Bruntcliffe Lane, Morley, LS27 9LR; T: 0800 7832989;
E: sales@cooperhillbrewery.co.uk; 🅕 *@cooperhillbrewery*

Trinity Brewery, established in a disused toilet block of Wakefield's rugby
league stadium, was one of the remarkable stories of this book's first
edition. Now renamed, relocated and replenished with new fermenters
and conditioning tanks, the
brewery's story continues
through a growing range
of core cask ales of
moderate strength,
including the light and
zesty **Blonde** (3.8%), the
buttery, malty **Best** (3.8%)

and the more bitter refreshing **Seven Hills IPA** (4.5%). A selection of
seasonal ales broadens the choice still further.

Cold Bath Brewing Co

46 King's Road, Harrogate, HG1 5JW; T: 0330 880 7009;
W: coldbathbrewing.com; E: hi@coldbathbrewing.com;
⬛ *@coldbathbrewingco;* ⬛ *@coldbathbrewco;* ⬛ *@coldbathbrewing*

Having opened just prior to the pandemic, a craft ale taproom in the heart of Harrogate is now home to a brewery focused on creating delicate, balanced beers which blend Yorkshire ingredients with a dash of Europe's finest hops.

The brewery is on a mezzanine above the bar and produces a core range which includes a crisp, floral continental style **Lager** (4.2%) and a substantially fruity but sessionable **Pale** (3.8%).

Several of their recipes show an imaginative touch. The classic Bavarian **Pilsner** (5.2%) is mashed with cobble loaves from Bettys tearoom, while the **IPA** (5.2%) has a distinct continental feel, deriving significant citric flavour and some real sharpness from its cocktail of four hops, lager malt and Belgian farmhouse and wine yeasts.

The beautiful taproom and brewhouse are home to an experimental oak barrel-aged project which caters to the connoisseurs with an apricot and nectarine **Saison** (6.6%) aged in a white-wine barrel and a beautifully rich and warming **Baltic Porter** (10%) aged and blended in rum and sherry barrels.

Copper Dragon

Snaygill Industrial Estate, Keighley Road, Skipton, BD23 2QR;
T: 01756 243243; W: copperdragon.co.uk; E: ruth@copperdragon.co.uk;
🅕 *@copperdragonbrewery;* 🅧 *@news_copper*

"We grew too fast," admits Steve Taylor, looking back on how Copper Dragon exploded onto the scene in the first decade of the Millennium, its breathtaking rise powered by the soaraway success of a single blonde ale, **Golden Pippin**. At first the brewery rode the crest of this considerable wave, before sliding into financial difficulties. This tale might have remained just a cautionary note to others but for the Taylor family's determination to remain in the industry – and their indignation at others attempting to trade on the brewery's good name.

As battle raged over the future of Copper Dragon, the family even established an independent cuckoo brewer called Recoil, to get back into the game. "We didn't know how long it was going to take, so that was a contingency," explains Steve's son Matthew.

And after a long legal tussle over the rights to the products, Copper Dragon is finally back on the up, albeit more slowly and cautiously this time around. Re-establishing their customer base has been firstly a case of assuring them that theirs is the real deal: "We had to literally knock on the door of every public house," says Steve.

After a period brewing in Keighley, this famous Yorkshire brewery finally returned to its spiritual home in Skipton in 2020, with Matthew stepping up as Managing Director and Head Brewer.

Amber-coloured **Best Bitter** (3.8%) is a refreshing beer of genuine taste and substance with a beguiling sweet aroma and some genuine bitter bite in the finish. Firm and malty **Scott's 1816** (4.1%) is given fruity sharpness by Slovenian and Styrian Goldings hops; pale straw-coloured **Silver Myst** (4%) is to all intents and purposes a German styled cask lager without the excessive carbonation of some big-name brands. Limited editions and seasonal ales extend the range; the familiar logo of a fearsome dragon guarding a copper brewing vessel makes them very easy to spot.

And though Copper Dragon's future is now settled, Recoil beers such as the blonde **Antidote** (3.8%) continue to find their way to market.

As we went to press, the beautifully-named pale ale **Grain of Thrones** (4.1%) had been launched to mark the coronation of King Charles III.

Steve and Matthew Taylor

Golden Pippin (3.9%)

This remains the Copper Dragon piece de resistance, a "go-to" beer for drinkers seeking a sessionable Yorkshire blonde. It has the clear golden colour that the name suggests, and though it has only a moderate wisp of lemon in the aroma, it bursts on the palate with a crisp, clean, tongue-cleansing burst of apple and gooseberry, before a long grapefruity aftertaste leaves you gagging for more. It is a Yorkshire legend, restored to greatness.

Craven Brew Co *New*

Station Road, Crosshills, Skipton, BD20 7DT; T: 01535 637451;
W: www.cravenbrew.co.uk; E: hello@cravenbrew.co.uk; **f** *@cravenbrewco*

Dave Sanders is one of Yorkshire's most celebrated brewers. Having begun his career with the Firkin brewpub chain, he has since added the likes of Elland, Kirkstall, Saltaire, Old Mill and Copper Dragon to his impressive CV. Small wonder then that these newbies honour their brewer with home-page status on their website.

Here, Dave concentrates his efforts on very traditional ales, marketed with some eye-catching pump clips and three-letter names. The light and easy-going session pale ale **SPA** (3.7%) is the entry to a range which gains progressive strength via best Yorkshire bitter **BYB** (3.8%), US-hopped 'extra fine ale' **EFA** (4.2%), rich black Angus porter **BAP** (4.5%) and the formidable golden Craven pale ale **CPA** (4.8%).

Right beside the brewery, the 12-tap Crosshills taproom showcases this whole range – as well as some of Dave's seasonal specials.

Crooked Brewing Limited

The Garages, Leeds East Airport, Church Fenton, LS24 9SE; T: 07890 526505;
W: crookedbrewing.co.uk; E: steve@crookedbrewing.co.uk;
🐦 *@crookedbrewltd;* 📷 *@crookedbrewing*

Have you heard the one about the Englishman, the Welshman, the Irishman and the Zimbabwean? This unlikely quartet established this microbrewery in 2017 at the former Church Fenton RAF base which has now been re-invented as Leeds East Airport.

Most Crooked beers don't get further than their own tap in Acomb, which has an ever-changing line-up, but almost always includes the well-balanced session ale **Spokes** (4%), to which Amarillo and Cascade hops lend some interesting citric notes. Saaz hops work their central European magic on **Lager Lager Lager** (4.2%), while rich Ecuadorian Cacao drops lend a wonderful elegance to the dangerously powerful chocolate stout **Killing Me Softly** (6.2%).

A second brewery tap in Driffield is likely to soak up much of the remaining production from this wonderful under-the-radar addition to the local scene.

Daleside Brewery

Camwal Road, Starbeck, Harrogate, HG1 4PT; T: 01423 880022;
W: dalesidebrewery.com; E: enquiries@dalesidebrewery.com;
f ♥ ◎ *@DalesideBrewery*

Daleside Brewery has been producing cask ales and bottled beers since the mid-1980s, a time when micro-brewing was in its infancy, and many of the signs were suggesting that traditional British beer could be in terminal decline. When Bill Witty established the brewery, he was something of an outlier pushing against the prevailing wind.

But it thrived then, and continues to do so. And it was here that renowned writer and brewer Garrett Oliver, the founder of New York's trendsetting behemoth Brooklyn Brewery – and editor of the equally heavyweight *Oxford Companion to Beer* – learned the basics of his trade.

Daleside's cask range focuses on quality easy drinking beers, such as **Daleside Blonde** (3.9%), a full-flavoured flaxen ale with a hoppy aroma, that remains popular across the brewery's heartland and beyond, and **Daleside Bitter** (3.7%) a classic English bitter, copper coloured with a refreshing, crisp malt finish. Strong, dark, bottled beers **Monkey Wrench** (5.3%) and **Morocco Ale** (5.5%) also have a keen following.

Late in 2022, the brewery produced a batch of its **Ruby Ale** (5.5%) in wooden casks for a festival at the Junction Inn in Castleford, organised by the Society of the Preservation of Beer from the Wood.

There is something of the fruit and nut about the cheekily-named, bright and effervescent copper-coloured **Old Leg Over** (4.1%). The whispered sweetness of dried fruit and almonds dominate a taste which is definitely more mild than bitter and deliciously easy drinking. Its malty, peaty nature develops further in the aftertaste and rather puts one in mind of a fine Scotch.

Daleside General Manager Adam Cox

🍺 Pacesetter (3.9%)

This refreshing, bright golden beer – a stronger version of a beer they retired some years ago – was an addition to the range in 2022, its label celebrating the county's latter-day love for road cycling, forged in 2014's Tour de France and strengthened in the years since by the Tour de Yorkshire. Gentle, easy-going Pacesetter might just be the thing after a long stint in the saddle – an enticing lemony aroma leads into a sunshine taste, a dash of ginger, a hint of oranges, all pinned to this slightly biscuity, modestly carbonated backbone. And the sessionable strength ensures you're easily seduced to have another.

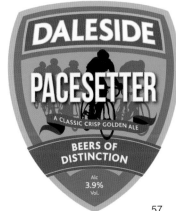

Dark Horse Brewery

Coonlands Laith, Hetton, BD23 6LY; T: 01756 730555;
W: darkhorsebrewery.co.uk; E: darkhorsebrewery@btinternet.com;
🅕 @ *darkhorsebrewery*

Owner Richard Eyton-Jones already had some impressive breweries on his CV – Goose Eye and Old Mill in Yorkshire, St Peter's and Old Cannon in Suffolk – before he and wife Carole established Dark Horse Brewery in pretty Hetton in 2008, using their own borehole for water. And since 2016, their four beers **Hetton Pale** (4.2%), **Craven Bitter** (3.8%), **Night Jar** (4.2%) and **Blonde Beauty** (3.9%) have become permanently available.

Hetton's renowned Angel Inn is perhaps the perfect place to sample these local brews, though they reach pubs across the Dales. These customers proved loyal during the pandemic: "Many have increased the number of beers they are taking from us," says Carole. "It's been amazing."

Hetton Pale Ale (4.2%)

This clean-tasting, slightly sweet and peachy pale ale could hardly have had a more favourable introduction; its inaugural brew won the ITV series *Yorkshire's Perfect Pint* in 2008. Available in bottle and cask, it continues to deliver on the uncomplicated values which took that prize. It pours an attractive golden colour with some seductive citrus in the aroma, before the deeper substance of malt and caramel emerge in the taste of a very easy-going Yorkshire ale.

Darkland Indie Brew Co

Unit 4C, Ladyship Business Park, Mill Ln, Halifax, HX3 6TA; T: 07714 344723;
W: darklandindiebrewco.com; E: info@darklandindiebrewco.com;
🅵 🅳 🅾 @darklandbrewery

A prize for the best porter-stout at the 2023 Bradford Beer Festival for their coconut and vanilla porter **Paradise** (4.8%) was the latest confirmation that this much-loved brewer was back in action, after a seeming hiatus which had seen their social media dormant, and web address re-directing to a photographer's site.

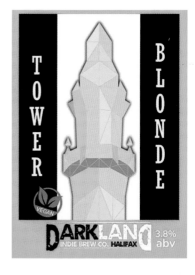

But a new website offers assurances that it's still up and running, albeit with a change of personnel and modest change of name – a fact confirmed by a trio of beers at CAMRA's members' weekend in April 2023. **Tower Blonde** (3.8%) is a nicely balanced malty pale, **Monterey** (4.5%) a classic dry-hopped West Coast IPA.

I'm not sure if this beer was produced under the old regime or the new, but the red-tinged, slightly tart fruit ale **Bohemian Raspberry** (3.8%) takes the prize for the best beer name of this edition of the *Yorkshire Beer Bible*.

4.8%
ABV   PARADISE   COCONUT & VANILLA STOUT

Dead Parrot Beer Co

44 Garden Street, Sheffield, S1 4BJ;
🐦 📷 *@DeadParrotBeer.*

Back in the 1980s, I spent ten weeks on a journalism course in Sheffield, where we soon discovered the Frog and Parrot, which was that vanishingly rare beast in those days, a brewpub. Drinking beer on the premises where it was brewed felt like an amazing experience.

The pub is long gone, but its name is remembered in this relative newcomer to the Sheffield scene, which opened in October 2018. Based in an old industrial unit near the city centre, brewer Mark Simmonite uses kit originally purchased for Aardvark Brewery, but never used.

His beers include the floral and biscuity **Aurornis Xui** (4.6%) and the liquorice and caramel stout **Kato Nwar** (4.8%). **Maranta** (4.5%) is a crisp lime and lemon pale.

And naming your blueberry pale ale **Norwegian Blue** (4.7%) should certainly attract fans of Monty Python to the stunning on-site taproom, Perch, which combines dark wood and leather fittings with its old red-brick industrial heritage to create an impressive venue of genuine industrial chic.

DMC Brewery  *New*

2A, Cliffe Hill Works, Balne Lane, Wakefield, WF2 0DF; W: dmcbrewery.com;
E: hello@dmcbrewery.com; 🅕 🅞 *@DMCBrewery*

Husband and wife Giuseppe (Gez) and Ele Romano first started making ginger beers in their kitchen as a Covid project; almost four years on, theirs is the only brewery in Britain concentrating on this niche. Disappointed by the lack of good quality alcoholic ginger beers on the market and sharing a natural passion and interest in brewing, they decided to make their own.

Using only fresh ginger root combined with natural ingredients to preserve the true flavours, Gez and Ele have created a range of gluten-free and vegan-friendly ginger beers brewed using natural ingredients and focused on bringing a genuine depth of flavour and clean, fresh, natural taste. Says brewery spokesman Tom Webster: "Whether it's drinking from a horn round an open fire, watching your favourite band at a gig, or swigging from a wooden tankard at a medieval event, DMC's ginger beers are perfect for any occasion!"

The entry-level beer is the straight-up ginger ale **OGB** (5.2%) which is brewed to an 18th-century recipe, but the range is extended through innovative combinations to enhance the flavour. Lemongrass and lime leaf lend their influence on **Arabia** (4.4%); cinnamon, orange and star anise give extra zest to **Valhalla** (4.5%) while cacao nibs and chilli bring richness and bite to the hazy amber and beautifully-refreshing **Chaac** (5%).

I was alarmed to read that uber-strong California Reaper chillies had been added to the recipe for **Ales From The Crypt** (5.5%) but their influence is limited to some extra warmth on the back of the throat, softened by the brew's dash of fresh pineapple. Two meads – the potent **Imperial Braggot** (10%) and less challenging **Cyser** (6%) flesh out the choice still further.

DMC bottles are gradually finding their way into

Ele and Gez Romano

specialist stores, while a mobile bar is allowing them to take their ginger message across the country to food festivals, gigs – and even battle reenactments: "It's probably our alternative aesthetic and our historic recipes, but we often find ourselves at events with a lot of swords and leather!" says Tom

Baron (5.5%)

This lovely ginger ale pours a flat hazy amber, with just a suggestion of cloves poking past the unmistakable ginger of the aroma. A very thin pale head soon dissipates, but Baron hits the palate with a huge ginger headrush that zips through the olfactory system, clearing the nasal passageways and warming the throat. There's a slight earthiness as it settles to its task, but a determined sweetness and chilli-like heat linger to leave you thirsty for more.

Doncaster Brewery

7 Young Street, Doncaster, DN1 3EL; T: 07921 970941;
W: doncasterbrewery.co.uk; E: brewer@doncasterbrewery.co.uk;
f 𝕏 *@donnybrewery*

The 2012 St Leger Festival saw the launch of a brewery built
from scratch over the course of nine months by engineer-
turned-brewer Ian Blaylock. He runs it with wife Alison; both
are Doncaster born and bred.

CHESWOLD
BITTER
Maris Otter malt and a single hop variety
of East Kent Gouldings. A fruity/spicy
aroma with a lingering spicy bitter
4.2% ABV

Their beers are sold to pubs in Hull, Sheffield, Doncaster,
Barnsley and through their excellent city-centre taproom,
which also boasts six traditional ciders, ten keg beers,
more than 150 European bottled beers, a range of gins
and a cracking wine list. The taproom has garnered a heap
of CAMRA awards, including being named Doncaster Pub
of the Year for the third year running in 2020.

The beers are named after things related to Doncaster –
people, places, historic events and of course locomotives.
They include the blonde **Sand House** (3.8%) and the
darker, sturdier **Cheswold** (4.2%). These are available in
bottle along with a range of occasional brews such as the
pale ale **St Georges Minster** (4%), the darker **Mucky
Bucket** (5%), **Stirling Single Breakfast Stout** (4.5%)
and **1194 Charter Porter** (5.5%).

SAND HOUSE
BLONDE
Golden straw coloured beer made with lager
and wheat malts, using cascade & summit
hops.
3.8% ABV

Eagles Crag Brewery

Unit 21, Robinwood Mill, Burnley Road, Todmorden, OL14 8HP;
T: 01706 810394; W: eaglescragbrewery.com;
E: sales@eaglescragbrewery.com; 🄵 🄾 *@eaglescrag brewery*

2022 was the 180th anniversary of The Great Strike – the biggest concerted workers' protest in Victorian England. Chiefly around wages and working conditions, the protests began in Staffordshire's coal mines and soon spread to Manchester, Leeds, Preston and to Halifax, where six people were killed in a riot. These momentous events are commemorated in the pale, golden and refreshing **Eagle's Strike** (4.2%), a worthy addition to the core range of a brewery whose beers are enjoyed in more than 200 outlets either side of the Pennines.

Brewers Dave Mortimer and Chris Milton bring over 30 years' brewing experience to their eight-barrel plant, named after a local landmark and based in an old textiles mill.

Their biggest seller is well-balanced citric **Pale Eagle** (4%) which has garnered a string of awards. Amber **The Eagle Has Landed** (4.6%) derives notable piney and floral flavours from Cascade, Chinook and Simcoe hops, and is balanced with some sturdy malt, while **Eagles Feather** (3.8%) is a paler, lighter take on the same recipe.

Firm, strong **Bald Eagle** (6.9%) draws bags of bitter pithy punch from Columbus, Citra and Mosaic, while deep ruby porter **The Eagle of Darkness** (5%) has some heady chocolate and coffee character. **Golden Eagle** (5%) is a generously-proportioned sharply citrus American-hopped blonde bombshell.

Many breweries do a changing pale, based on different combinations of hops; few have so splendid a name as **Alter Eagle** (4.5%).

There's a certain symbiosis between the brewery and the local ecosystem. Spent hops are used to improve soil fertility in planters around the town, spent yeast is put to work in local compost bins, and a nearby pork farm

fattens its pigs on Eagles Crag malt.

An on-site taproom is open on the last Friday and Saturday of each month; that the brewery is so well-loved is perhaps best demonstrated by the £4,000 raised by the local CAMRA branch to support them during the pandemic.

 Centurion Eagle (9.5%)
Strong dark meaty porters were exported from London to the Baltic states from the late 18th century – and gained their Imperial title due to the enthusiastic patronage of that lady of prodigious appetites, Czarina Catherine the Great. By the outbreak of the First World War – and certainly by the Russian Revolution three years later – this once lucrative trade route had all but dried up. For decades the

only British brewery retaining the name was John Smith's. It was this Tadcaster beer which ultimately sparked the revival of the style, its export to America re-awakening interest in these dark and seriously potent beers.

Just as many brewers have created all manner of India Pale Ales, so have several re-visited this genre too. The Eagle's Crag version is emblematic of a recent diversion into barrel ageing which has yielded remarkable success. Matured for five months in an oak whisky barrel, Centurion packs chocolate, coffee and some dangerous whisky notes into a surprisingly easy-drinking and beautifully warming stout.

A second barrel-ageing venture, **Regal Eagle** (8.5%), combined flaked and roasted barley, Maris Otter and chocolate malts, oats and English hops with similar results; a batch matured for 18 months was a treat for visitors to the Calderdale Beer and Cider Festival in September 2022.

Elland Brewery

Heathfield Industrial Estate, Elland, HX5 9AE; T: 01422 377677;
W: ellandbrewery.co.uk; E: info@ellandbrewery.co.uk; 🅕 🅣 *@ellandbrewery*

Two microbreweries came together to establish Eastwood and Sanders in 2002 – and despite changes of ownership, location and personnel, it continues to do all the important things consistently well. Best known for its **1872 Porter**, CAMRA's Champion Beer of Britain in 2013, Elland's core range has been slimmed down in the past few years to focus on the sharp **South Sea Pale** (4.1%), fruity best bitter **Nettle Thrasher** (4.4%) and restful and sessionable **Elland Blonde** (4%). A roster of seasonals shakes up the choice on a regular basis, while the nearby Elland Craft and Tap is the best place to sample the full range.

 1872 Porter (6.5%)

1872 was the year of the Mary Celeste, the first FA Cup Final – and the original recipe for this rich and treacly porter. You know you are in for a treat as soon as you start to pour the beer, releasing some enticing caramel. Almost opaque jet-black in the glass, it settles beneath a foaming ivory head, inviting you to dive in. Once there, your palate is bathed in a silky blanket abundant in the luxurious array of flavours symbolic of a great porter. There is dark chocolate, the bitterness of espresso, soft malt, red wine and a smokiness which lingers in the top of the mouth as a final sweetness slowly develops on the throat. It's wonderful – and if you can ever find it in a wooden cask, drink the lot.

Elvington Brewery *New*

Station Yard, Elvington, YO41 4EL; T: 01904 607197; W: elvingtonbrewery.co.uk

Well-established beer retailer Pivovar branched out into brewing in 2021, concentrating production on quality Czech-influenced lagers, initally for sale through their Pivni bar in York. Within months, crisp, clear **Mittels Pils** (4.4%) had underlined its authenticity by winning the trophy for the best keg lager at the International Brewing awards. Encouraged by the success, a sizeable expansion of capacity is bringing their beers to a wider audience.

Empire Brewing

The Old Boiler House, Unit 33, Upper Mills, Slaithwaite, HD7 5HA;
T: 01484 847343; E: empirebrewing@aol.com;
@ empire-brewing-company; @empirebrewinguk

The Beverley family's brewery began life in 2006 in a converted garage where the first brew was American-hopped pale ale **Strikes Back** (4%) which remains a part of the range to this day. They have since upped-sticks to a picturesque canalside location where they produce their thirst-quenching zesty session ale **Golden Warrior** (3.8%) and golden **Valour** (4.2%), among others.

A chance visit to the King's Head in Huddersfield in March 2023 allowed me to sample their wonderful Milk **Chocolate Stout** (6%) – fortified with cacao nibs and barrel-aged for six months. Fabulous.

Farmers beers cheek-by-jowl with stablemates from Haworth

Farmers Arms and Brewing Co

Muker, Richmond, DL11 6QG; T: 01748 866297; W: farmersarmsmuker.co.uk;
E: farmersmuker@gmail.com

The Gascoigne family has owned a small microbrewery for thirty years
– and it has travelled with them from the Scottish isles, to Yorkshire's
industrial heartlands, and now to Swaledale, where the family has added
the Farmers Arms to a portfolio which also includes the lovely Haworth
Steam Brewing bar (see page 86).

Rather than push his beers out far and wide through wholesalers,
brewer Andy Gascoigne concentrates on relatively low-volume cask ales,
sold exclusively through the two pubs, though some does make its way
into bottle.

The names of the beers emphasise their local credentials. Softly-
spoken IPA **Crackpot** (4%) references a curiously-named village nearby;
crisp blonde **Shepherdess** (4.2%) honours Swaledale farmer Amanda
Owen whose trials and tribulations made for compelling TV. Firm and
luxurious **Gundog** (4.5%) is a wonderful black velvet sensation, its name
a nod to the farmers and gamekeepers who maintain an important local
pastime.

Fernandes Brewery

5 Avison Yard, Kirkgate, Wakefield, WF1 1UA; T: 07949 833138;
W: luisbar.co.uk; E: luisbarwakefield@hotmail.com;
🎯 *@luisbaratfernandesbrewery;* 🐦 📷 *@luisbarwakefield*

Established as a brewpub in 1997, the exotic-sounding Fernandes was one of the early names in the vanguard of Yorkshire's brewing revolution, bringing to this former maltstore an exciting taste of things to come.

Though still on the same premises – where a lack of mains drainage means that all the waste water has to be manhandled to the drains – Fernandes has recently won its independence after being owned by local heavyweight Ossett Brewery for a decade.

Under its new ownership, the pub upstairs serves an ever-changing selection of nine cask ales, including many from the Fernandes range, each distinguished by their wonderfully artistic pump clips. They include old favourites like dry and chocolatey **Malt Shovel Mild** (3.8%), smooth and sessionable **Ale To The Tsar** (4.1%) and robust roasted malt **Double Six** (6%). Mind you, with more than 30 different brews on its roster, Fernandes offers the curious drinker almost endless choice.

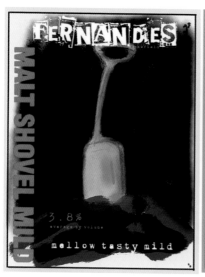

Fuggle Bunny Brewhouse

1, Meadowbrook Park Industrial Estate,
Halfway, Sheffield, S20 3PJ;
T: 07949 133211;
W: fugglebunnybrewhouse.co.uk;
E: info@fugglebunny.co.uk;
🅯 🅭 @fugglebunny

Fuggle Bunny's innovative marketing strategy marries a story about an inquistive rabbit called Fuggle to a catalogue of quality beers, taking a radical approach to getting noticed. Each of the brewery's beers is a chapter in the story, the ingredients used are weaved into the story as the products of one bunny's search for beery excellence.

The story starts with the malty, sweetish amber **New Beginnings** (4.9%) and progresses via the more markedly hoppy and citric **Cotton Tail** (4%), the big-selling moderately bitter IPA **24 Carrot** (6%) and the imperial stout **Russian Rarebit** (5%).

Its newest episode, the full-bodied, fruit and vanilla IPA **Stomper** (5%), is the first to be written by Matt and Laura Hadgkiss who took over here during the pandemic. They initially sold beer in growlers and bag-in-boxes, and filled up whatever containers customers brought to their on-site taproom in the south-eastern suburbs of Sheffield. "We had people queueing around the block," says Matt.

They've now returned the focus to cask ales. They can often be found in free houses across Yorkshire, Derbyshire and Nottinghamshire and supply a number of Wetherspoon pubs across the region.

Goose Eye Brewery

Unit 5, Castlefields Industrial Estate, Crossflatts, BD16 2AF;
T: 01274 512743; W: goose-eye-brewery.co.uk;
E: info@goose-eye-brewery.co.uk; 🅵 🆇 *@gooseyebrewery*

Several members of the Atkinson family work at this popular brewery which was one of the pioneering new-generation micros when it opened in 1991, and relocated from Keighley to a custom-built brewery in nearby Crossflatts in 2017. Rooted in the traditional end of the market, their real ales include the more-ish American light ale **Spring Wells** (3.6%), roasted malt and chocolatey mild **Black Moor** (3.9%), premium strength English bitter **Pommie's Revenge** (5.2%) and the big-bodied fruit and liquorice **Over and Stout** (5.2%). The massively hopped and grapefruity **Chinook Blond** (4.2%) demonstrates a willingness to move with the times, and remains their biggest seller.

Gorilla Brewing

Unit 3, Cliff Street, Canalside Industrial Estate, Mexborough, S64 9HU;
T: 07747 484368; W: gorillabrewing.co.uk; 🅵 *@GorillaBrewingCoLtd;*
🆇 *@BrewingGorilla;* 🅾 *@gorilla_brewingco*

This six-barrel brewery opened in 2020, taking over the premises of the former Don Valley Brewery. Here an on-site taproom dispenses simian delights such as the well-balanced, gentle tropical blonde ale **Silverback** (3.8%), the zesty, fruity golden **Orang-a-Tang** (4.5%) and hop-heavy IPA **Kong** (6%).

Great British Breworks

34 Dove Way, Kirkby Mills Industrial Estate, Kirkbymoorside,
North Yorks, YO62 6QR; T: 01751 433111; W: gbbreworks.co.uk;
E: info@breworks.co.uk

When brewer Tristan Hall began producing beer in the old wash house at Pickering's Black Swan pub, he revived a tradition which stretches back at least to Victorian times, though the last brewery here closed before the First World War.

Like a domestic house-moving chain, Rooster's move to Harrogate enabled Turning Point to take over their old premises in Knaresborough – enabling Breworks to expand to their former 12-barrel plant in Kirkbymoorside, massively increasing capacity.

Though Tristan's beers reach pubs around the area, the Black Swan remains the best place to try the range. Cask ales include the light and golden, fruity, buttery **Istanbul Pale Ale** (4.3%) and the bready, caramelly **Great Scot** (3.9%), which marked a visit by the Flying Scotsman to the North Yorkshire Moors Railway.

Coal Porter (4.9%)

This substantial, cocoa-endowed, and beautifully-named porter draws across the tongue a comfortable eiderdown of red wine, dark chocolate and liquorice. Fabulous – and a great name too.

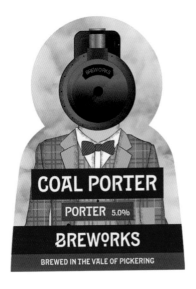

Great Newsome Brewery

Great Newsome Farm, South Frodingham, Hull, HU12 0NR; T: 01964 612201; W: greatnewsomebrewery.co.uk; E: enquiries@greatnewsomebrewery.co.uk; 🄵 🄾 *@greatnewsomebrewery;* 🄳 *@greatnewsome*

Doubling capacity by commissioning a new brewhouse was a sign of Great Newsome's progress over a first decade and a half. Opening it in January 2020 was spectacularly unfortunate timing.

Four generations of the Hodgson family have farmed the fertile soil of Holderness, roughly halfway between the suburbs of Hull and the bracing, windswept, shifting spit of the Spurn coast. Since diversifying into brewing they have garnered an enviable reputation for beers such as the sweetish **Liquorice Lads Stout** (4.3%) and an ever-changing seasonal range inspired by butterflies found on the farm, such as the light amber **Peacock** (4.5%) and the traditional IPA **Skipper** (4.8%).

The silky, amber, biscuit-scented **Frothingham Best** (4.3%) distributes lavish warming malt and the bitterness of berries and green apples in roughly equal measure. A silver medal at the 2022 World Beer Awards was just one of a string of prizes it has collected. Fresh and malty **Gatekeeper** (4.5%) whose grassy aroma is a showcase for Northern Brewer hop, was a new special in the spring of 2023.

And despite the pandemic coming as he unveiled his new brewhouse, director Matthew Hodgson wasn't to be deterred: "I was determined that we wouldn't shut down or mothball the brewery until things came good," he says. By developing their online sales, they maintained a brisk trade with orders going nationwide.

"And as a result of us always being here and serving our customers, we have come out stronger and in a better position for the future."

Honouring the local dialect name for a hedgehog, **Pricky Back Otchan** (4.2%) is a lemony, nutty, ale whose significant substance lends the impression of something a good deal more potent. The batch of this popular beer brewed in April 2023 marked the 2,400th brew for Great Newsome – enough beer, they calculated, to fill an Olympic-sized swimming pool, Withernsea Pavilion Pool, 15 double-decker buses, 263,000 jam jars and the fuel tank of 4,500 Ford Fiestas. I'm not sure whether they actually plan to do this…

Sleck Dust (3.8%)

The first time I tried this, I was expecting something smoky, dirty and dark, perhaps subliminally imagining "sleck dust" to be the thick black air, pregnant with coal dust breathed in by colliers working the seam.

It turns out that the dust referenced here is actually something thrown up on Yorkshire's sunny smiling surface, rather than its dark-hearted underground. Earlier incarnations of the label offer a clue, showing a combine harvester reaping the grain on a sun-kissed summer's day – no doubt stirring a fug of dust into the air as it goes.

No matter, Sleck Dust proves to be pale blonde with a thick white head, some pithy zest in the aroma and a refreshing, slightly floral taste, with some bready, yeasty notes, all zipped around by some significant carbonation.

Grizzly Grains Brewing New

Unit 6, Duchess Rd, Sheffield, S2 4BB; T: 07807 242545;
E: sambrewsbeers@gmail.com; 🇫 *@grizzlygrainsbrewing;* 🅾 *@grizzly_grains*

Having released his first beer in January 2020, Sam Bennett saw his business plans immediately derailed by Covid. Switching to 'bag-in-a-box' for home deliveries, he kept things moving and as he glimpsed the light at the end of the lockdown tunnel, bought the brewkit from Crosspool Alemakers and decamped to an industrial unit close to Sheffield United's Bramall Lane ground.

From here, his cask beers make their way into pubs around the city, and sometimes further afield. "We don't really have a core range," he says. "We brew an ever-changing set of beers – some do get repeated but not often enough to be considered core."
They include the smooth and sweetish, coffee, chocolate and toffee stout **Tilt Hammer** (4.9%), one of many Sheffield beers which doff their cap to the city's steelmaking heritage.

A huge malt bill of 11 different malts from UK, Belgium and Germany went into the mash which created the full-bodied dark mild **Big Dimples** (3.4%), which was brewed as a parti-gyle – essentially where the mash is used to make more than one beer – alongside an imperial stout. **Get On** (4.5%) is part of Sam's Get series of hazy Citra-driven pale ales, each using an American hop for dry-hopping; here it's El Dorado.

The gently spicy and banana-accented **Autobarn** (4.5%) a very decent take on a traditional German hefeweizen; locally-grown quinces and crab apples lend an imaginative twist to his Farmhouse Saison series.

Clearly one for variety, Sam has already collaborated with Derbyshire's Torside Brewery and near-neighbours Little Critters, while his sparkling **Sheffield Mead** (9.5%) made with local honey, added a further string to the Grizzly Grains bow. A new taproom, which opened for the first time early in 2023, is the best place to discover what he turns his hand to next.

TORRSIDE BREWING

GRIZZLY GRAINS BREWING

a Torrside/ Grizzly Grains collaboration

Big Words

olicana & cascade pale

4.8%

Unfined
Unfiltered

QUINCE FARMHOUSE
SAISON

Guisborough Brewery

14 South Buck Way, Guisborough, TS14 7FJ; T: 07703 002858;
W: guisboroughbrewery.co.uk; E: info@guisboroughbrewery.co.uk;
⬤ 🔲 ⬤ *@guisbrew*

Robin Field has enjoyed a varied career, with stints as a beach lifeguard, a primary school teacher and working on TV cooking programmes with chefs Gary Rhodes and Rick Stein.

"I grew up with an appreciation of proper beer, especially coming from West Cornwall where Skinner's was making ground alongside the well-established St Austell and Sharp's." This love deepened while he studied at Bristol University and later worked in television, where beer was the catalyst for great programme ideas "written on the back of an envelope in the pub."

But the seed of setting up the brewery was actually sown years later when he took his family for a "life break" in Western Australia, where a friend introduced him to the local breweries. "Often the brewer would ask how many breweries there were, where we lived. And in Saltburn, Redcar and Cleveland there were very few. The idea of setting up a brewery took hold."

Back home, Robin found a unit on a new industrial estate in Guisborough and bought a five-barrel brewkit from a brewery in Ireland whose best known beer was a red ale. "In January 2020 we did our first brew, **Phoenix** (4%), a red ale in homage to the kit's new lease of life. One silver lining of the pandemic was that people looked to support local businesses and so I was able to build a local following and online presence."

Since then he has established a rotating range: "All of them come round again, but some more often than others."

Powered by Centennial and Amarillo hops, the dry and assertively bitter session IPA **Daze** (4.3%) punches way above its weight, the gentle lemony notes of the aroma soon masked by its chunky, chewy malt character. Barely any light creeps through the black-hearted depths of hazelnut porter **Nut Kin** (4.5%) which has a sweet milk chocolate aroma before treading lightly across the palate, all nuts, wood smoke and dark fruit.

Six malts combine in the big-bodied stout **Rock Steady** (5%) which is as strong a beer as Robin is keen to make: "Regardless of what's in front of me, I drink at the same pace and that best suits a session beer, hence all of my beers so far are between 3.7% and 5%. Ultimately I brew beers that I enjoy and if others do as well then all the better."

His latest is the **Hinterland** Kolsch (4.5%) which was brewed to mark the 50th anniversary of a local football club.

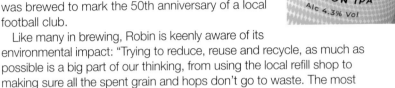

Like many in brewing, Robin is keenly aware of its environmental impact: "Trying to reduce, reuse and recycle, as much as possible is a big part of our thinking, from using the local refill shop to making sure all the spent grain and hops don't go to waste. The most environmentally-friendly way to buy beer is directly from your local brewery."

A taproom on site gives customers that option, and there's a fair chance you might bump into Brian, a regular customer whose misadventures include having to remove a pair of super strong magnets from a colleague's long hair with scissors, and inadvertently bringing back radioactive material from a holiday. He is honoured by the jet-black chilli stout **Dangerous Brian** (5%) which has some suggestions of liquorice on the nose, black pepper and blackcurrant notes in a complex taste, and the sharp warming bite of chilli in a finish which lasts and lasts.

Robin, who continues to teach maths part-time, stresses the importance of education in what he does: "I like to bring people together to help educate them about real beer and its heritage – and try and create as many 'I met someone in the pub the other day' moments as possible."

BOBA (5%)

Guisborough is among Yorkshire's most northerly breweries, so it makes sense to brew a style of beer most commonly associated with those heathens over the border in Tyneside. BOBA stands for Big Old Brown Ale, and this is a gentle sweetish caramelly take on a genre which has been seemingly pushed to the margins amid the explosion of beer styles championed by the craft ale revolution. There are some soft whisky-ish notes to the aroma of a beautfully translucent deep amber beer, which glides across the palate, all malty toffee goodness.

Half Moon Brewery

Forge House, Ellerton, York, YO42 4PB; T: 01757 288977;
W: halfmoonbrewery.co.uk; E: info@halfmoonbrewery.co.uk;
🅕 *@halfmoonbrewery;* 🐦 *@halfmoonbrewer;* 📷 *@halfmoon_brewer*

Tony Rogers worked in engineering and IT for many years, while quietly honing his skills as a home brewer. Now, behind sage-green garage doors in this cul-de-sac village south of York, and using tanks salvaged from a shampoo factory, his 5.5-barrel brewery produces an interesting choice of beers which are distributed across Yorkshire in cask and bottle.

Until 1969, this was the blacksmith's workshop, a fact honoured by the flagship beer, the amber, lightly spiced and lemony **Old Forge Bitter** (3.9%).

Gwei-Lo Beer

Unit 6, Enterprise Complex, Walmgate, York, YO1 9TT; W: gweilobeer.co.uk;
E: sales@gweilobeer.co.uk; 🅕 🐦 📷 *@gweilobeeruk*

The Cantonese name literally translates as "ghost people" and is a commonly-used slang term for westerners. The brewery was established in Hong Kong in 2014, and is now the island's biggest, with 70% of the market share – and is a significant exporter, notably to Australia. To allow further expansion, Gwei-Lo is now cuckoo brewing in Vietnam and Belgium, as well as at Brew York, with big plans for the US and Canada in the pipeline.

"Fun beers and fruited sours are our big thing," says boss Ian Jebbitt, sporting a gaudy multicoloured jacket to promote his sweetish **Rainbow Sherbet Sour** (4.5%). **Totally Tropical** (6.5%) is a heavily coconut-accented sour, while **Neon Jungle** (5.9%) is a fruit-laden IPA. "Every UK brewery is chasing the same market," says Ian. "We're trying to do something different."

Ian Jebbitt and Harry Mellor promoting Rainbow Sherbet Sour at Leeds International Beer Festival in 2022.

Jackie and Tony Rogers

And though Tony always has a porter or stout, an IPA and a couple of pale ales available, the range changes all the time. I'm lucky enough to have tried several: American Cascade hops lend a significant blast of grapefruit to **F'Hops Sake** (3.9%), while Bramling Cross adds dark berry notes and a rounded, fruity bitterness to **Blonde** (4.2%). At Christmas watch out for multi-hopped IPA **Blitzen** (4.3%) and **Figgy Pudding** (5.2%), a luxuriant dark porter full of figs and all things nice, while the bright **Honeymoon** (4.8%), with its sweet undertones of local unpasteurised honey, plays to the lunar theme.

Hazy golden **Wakatu** (5.8%), a bold IPA powered by the New Zealand hop of the same name, was the favourite beer of those at a Yorkshire Beer Tasting I held in Leeds in late 2021.

Tony's wife Jackie is also a partner in the business: "During lockdown we put up a new website and online shop and also started producing bottle-conditioned beers available in the shop. We're also doing tap nights on the last Friday of the month from April to September."

Dark Masquerade (3.6%)

Despite its moderate strength, this full-bodied brown ale – a permanent feature of the Half Moon range – is a robust cocktail of dark chocolate, cloves, bitter orange marmalade and liquorice. The aroma is not unlike that of a wheat beer and there's something of that clovey, banana experience on the palate, before some earthy bitterness and interesting smoky notes emerge in the finish. On a visit to Half Moon's tiny taproom the beer was being imaginatively served with segments of Guppy's Chocolate Orange Shards – a good match.

Halifax Steam Brewing Company

The Conclave, Southedge Works, Hipperholme, Halifax, HX3 8EF;
T: 07506 022504; W: halifax-steam.co.uk; E: info@halifax-steam.co.uk;
f *@halifaxsteam;* **𝕏** *@cockothenorth;* **◎** *@halifax-steam-brewery-tap*

Though founded as recently as 1999, this is now Calderdale's oldest brewery. Originally based in Brighouse, in 2002 the brewery moved a few miles up the A644 to Hipperholme, where a five-barrel plant produces a changing range of beers which are predominantly sold through their own Cock O' The North pub on the same site. **Uncle Jon** (4.3%) is a nicely rounded, malty dark brown ale; there are bags of citric character in the golden **Childcatcher** (4.8%), while light and refreshing **Selene** (4%) is a simple fruity thirst-quencher.

Hambleton Brewery

Melmerby Green Rd, Melmerby, Ripon, HG4 5NB; T: 01765 640108;
W: hambletonbrewery.co.uk; E: office@hambletonbrewery.co.uk;
f ◎ *@hambletonbrewery*

The famous White Horse of Kilburn remains the emblem of a trailblazing brewery originally established by Nick Stafford at the bottom of his in-laws' garden more than thirty years ago. The equine theme continues into core beers such as the easy-drinking blonde **Stud** (4.3%) and the sessionable IPA **Thoroughbred** (5%).

The aptly-named porter **Nightmare** (5%) began life when Nick began a new brew one morning only to realise that he didn't have all the ingredients. Even so, the ale he cobbled together wasn't bad – it was the first winner of CAMRA's Winter Champion Beer of Britain award and remains one of his best-known beers, blending four malts into a full-on treacle, orange and chocolate delight.

Most of this range is also available in bottle alongside two gluten- and wheat-free beers, the pale ale **GFA** (4.8%) and lager **GFL** (5.2%). **Bootleggers** IPA (5%) namechecks a local covers band.

In recent times, the choice has expanded through a canning range which includes the uber-sessionable light ale **Green Star** (3%), crisp Yorkshire lager **Cavalla** (4.6%) and the hazy IPA **Diavolo** (4.7%), in which the juicy fruit character suggested by the label is nicely counterbalanced by some genuine bitterness.

As the former operations director of SIBA, Nick helped bring a host of other small brewers into the marketplace; the Melmerby brewery has small-scale bottling and canning lines used by other small breweries across Yorkshire and beyond.

Stallion Amber (4.2%)
The cold-eyed stare of the fearsome beast in close-up on the label suggests that this might be a dangerous ride, but this particular Stallion is tame enough to lead the drinker down a well-trodden path to the past. Though styled an amber ale, this is a delicious, keenly-hopped take on a traditional best bitter, full of flavour and packed with rich malt character – smooth, mollifying and distinguished.

Harrogate Brewing Co

Unit 7, Hookstone Centre, Hookstone Chase, Harrogate, HG2 7HW;
T: 07774 891664; W: harrogatebrewery.co.uk; E: info@harrogatebrewery.co.uk;
🐦 @harrogatebrewco; 🄵 @HarrogateBrewingCo; 🄾 @harrogate_brewing_co

When Joe and Julie Joyce took over Harrogate Brewing in January 2020, the timing could scarcely have been worse, coming just weeks before the pandemic visited havoc on an entire industry.

The brewery is barely a decade old, having been established in 2013 by former photographer Anton Stark and wife Sarah, and quickly gaining an enviable reputation in and around the spa town. An American-influenced IPA was their first; selling it in the town's splendid Old Bell Tavern put the new brewery in position-A for attracting immediate attention.

The new owners took the pandemic as an opportunity to adapt: "It spurred us on into establishing an online shop, so we're now able to offer nationwide delivery as well as local," says the couple's daughter Julie, one of several family members with an active role in the venture. Their son Matthew works in sales, and son-in-law Liam McCarthy is in charge of the brewing operation.

And it's continuing to thrive: "We've expanded our kit from 2.5 to 10 barrels and developed a number of new beers. While we still use glass bottles for many of our beers we have also invested in a canning machine which offers flexibility and a quick turnaround," says Julie. "This works really well when we have small-batch experimental brews or if we create a bespoke beer for a local business."

A rebrand, using a capital H inspired by local viaducts and an image of the Red Kite is reflected in a taproom which now has a permanent bar featuring beers from across the brewery's range. They include the traditional English-hopped **Cold Bath Gold** (4.4%) and mysterious, sulphurous **Horse Head Stetson** (5.9 %). The pale and piney **Stray All Day IPA** (4.6%) references the historic 200-acre parkland which stretches across the south and east of the spa town.

And while the taproom was previously just an occasional feature, music events, open-mic nights, jam sessions and visiting food vans have now

placed the venue right at the heart of its rather up-market east Harrogate community.

New brews have emerged with the change of regime, like **Harrogate Best Bitter** (4.5%) which recently won gold medals at both the regional and national SIBA beer awards.

Two new beers namecheck younger members of this new brewing dynasty. The heavyweight double dry-hopped New England IPA **Iris** (6.3%) was launched in 2021 to mark the arrival of Liam and Julie's daughter. The birth of Louis a year later was celebrated with the plummy, dark fruit tropical stout **Louis Louis** (6%). Both are part of the brewery's Happy Town range of distinctively hazy and hoppy beers.

Plum Porter (4.8%)
The earth-brown depths of this luxurious multi-award-winning ale throws off the kind of enticing damson aroma which would delight any WI jam-maker. There is some chocolate to the taste, and some autumnal, dark fruit character, but its sweetness is modest and never dominates this beautiful example of a full-bodied but sessional porter.

A family business – Kelly Gascoigne is a friendly face behind the bar at Haworth Steam Brewery

Haworth Steam Brewery

98 Main St, Haworth, BD22 8DP; T: 01535 646059;
W: haworthsteambrewery.co.uk; E: haworthsteambrew@gmail.com;
🅵 🅓 *@haworthsteam*

An attractive bar and bistro, set right at the top of Haworth's historic cobbled street, is the shopfront for a family-run operation which draws a brisk trade from locals and tourists alike.

Even so, owner Andy Gascoigne now brews his beers nearly 40 miles away at the Farmers Arms and Brewing Company in Muker (see page 69).

Perhaps his best-known product is the traditional, firm and bitter pale ale **Willie Eckerslike** (4.2%), the name a dialect response to the oft-asked question of whether the family would leave Haworth, amid a series of challenges, not least subsidence and rampant woodworm, which afflicted the premises and saw them closed for more than a year.

They didn't – and the lovely brewery tap has now been passed to daughter Kelly, who oversees a bar whose choice changes regularly to reflect Dad's eclectic range of relatively low-alcohol beers. These include the low-octane IPA **Hurricane** (3.6%), full-bodied amber bitter **Tyke** (3.8%) and zesty, refreshing, summery barley blonde **Over Yonder** (4.2%). **Nah Then** (4%) is a crisp, slightly fruity Yorkshire blonde.

Andy also brews two similarly-named lagers. **Vier** (4.1%) is a malty brew using German hops and English lager yeasts, the more substantial **Viper** (5%) a dry, clean-tasting pilsner.

The Gascoignes have invested heavily in the current popularity of gin, and make no fewer than 10 different varieties, some branded as Haworth Gin and some as the Miss Mollies sweetshop range, as well as their own tonics and mixers.

The bar serves hand-pulled cask ales from across the Haworth and Farmers range. It's the perfect place to visit after a day spent browsing the town's interesting shops or immersing yourself in the world of the Brontë sisters – the parsonage, the church and the graveyard. On my last visit, Kelly had pasted cuttings from past issues of the *Yorkshire Beer Bible* on the walls. Hopefully this one will make it up there too.

 Hells Bells (4.1%)

This firm and dry blonde ale is a recent addition to the Haworth roster. Cascade and Centennial hops lend some dense citric notes to the nose of a determinedly bitter ale, which develops further depth and dryness in the aftertaste. It's a sessionable beer – but one still packed with substance and character.

Heist Brew Co *New*

107 Neepsend Lane, Sheffield, S3 8AT; W: heistbrewco.com;
E: support@heistcraft.com; 🅕 🅧 🅘 *@heistbrew*

Though new to Yorkshire, Heist began life in 2018 in an old school classroom in Clowne, Derbyshire. "Our bar and bottle shop was looking for a brewery to rent some space that we had," explains co-founder Adam France. "A number of breweries came to look, but eventually we decided to simply do it ourselves."

Adam was as surprised as anyone when their first large-scale brew, the sweet milk stout **Pirate Material** (6%) proved a success: "To our disbelief it actually worked, tasted pretty damn good and rated really well – and that got us hooked."

From there the trajectory has pointed impressively upwards: "Don't get me wrong, we've had some massive failures through the years," says Adam. "We've brewed some stanking beers that bombed, but we've moved on, we've lived and we've learned."

They moved over the county line a couple of years ago to take up a 600-square-metre site in Sheffield, which has seen brewing capacity rise to 9,000 litres a week, while a taproom showcasing 30 beer lines, pub games and food draws a regular crowd.

Though the range builds in strength from the easy-going refreshing fruity Kolsch **Dead Storage** (4.3%), haze seems a consistent theme. Murky pale yellow-beige **Ray's Solero** (6.5%) is almost a fruit soda, a rich cocktail of passion fruit mango and papayas. The warming characteristics of the firm blast of peach schnapps bitterness from the rich and gloopy, sweet-smelling **Pablo's Hippos** (8.5%) more than compensates for its naked lack of subtlety.

From a tiny schoolroom with novice brewers to a cavernous site with international distribution – and all achieved in the face of a global pandemic – it's a remarkable story.

🍺 Marmalade Fingers (5.4%)

Perhaps more than any new beer I have tried during the preparation of this third edition of the *Yorkshire Beer Bible*, Marmalade Fingers has demonstrated that IPA is now so broad a church that the label is now almost meaningless.

Thirty years ago, India Pale Ale was a term largely confined to just a handful of brewers maintaining a proud British tradition for the original heavily-hopped ales once exported to slake the thirsts of the soldiers of the Raj.

Yet from the Big Bang of Derbyshire's Jaipur – and the relentless invention of brewers on America's east coast – the whole universe of IPA has expanded exponentially and there seems little sign of deceleration. It is now a badge that all brewers must apply to at least one of their beers, however little they happen to resemble those fabulous London and Burton originals.

A dirty, murky straw colour, Marmalade Fingers lurks in the glass like some unpleasant, pungent stranger waiting to step out of the dusk. The aroma is bitter oranges and this dry tart tang persists into a taste packed with bitterness – a twist of pine, a hint of danger. It's a wonderful, beguiling concoction, but drinking this blind, you might easily convince yourself that this is far stronger than 5.4%.

Helmsley Brewing Co

18 Bridge St, Helmsley, YO62 5DX; T: 01439 771014;
W: helmsleybrewingco.co.uk; E: kyle@helmsleybrewingco.co.uk;
🌐 🐦 @helmsleybrewing

An on-site bar and shop attracts a steady stream of visitors to a brewery which opened in 2014 and is already a favourite in the pubs of the old North Riding. English, Australian and Slovenian hops are blended into the attractive sunny **Helmsley Honey** (4.5%), but it is the two different wild flower and heather honeys, both sourced from the North York Moors National Park which dominate both its floral aroma and graceful, luxurious taste.

Dry flaxen bitter **Striding the Riding** (4%) is the official beer of the Cleveland Way and I came across it during a trip to the Forresters Arms in Kilburn, which is one of the early pub stops in this 110-mile scenic trek through the national park and down the Yorkshire coast. Other Helmsley beers include zesty **Howardian Gold** (4.2%) and the sparky tropical fruit pale ale **HiPA!** (5.5%).

Smoky, chocolatey **Jacky Boy** (5.5%) is cut from rather different cloth: the pour is languid and oily, the jet-black beer settles beneath a creamy

tan head from which some subtle coffee notes emerge. But such modesty disperses when Jacky Boy hits the palate in a headlong rush of treacle, toffee, milky coffee and dark chocolate. The addition of oatmeal to the brew lends body and substance; a cocktail of malts drives the taste, given just a little spike of sharpness by the hop content, before dusty, smoky flavours decorate a long aftertaste.

🍺 Yorkshire Legend (3.8%)

This deep russet-coloured ale blends five local malts into a toasty, caramelly, well-balanced ale which delivers all the complexity and easy-drinking character you would expect of a traditional Yorkshire bitter. Like many of the Helmsley beers, this is available in both cask and bottle.

Hilltop Brewing

Sheffield Rd, Conisbrough, Doncaster, DN12 2AY; T: 01709 868811

The Hilltop Hotel, a former Doncaster pub of the year, established a brewhouse in the rear yard a few years ago. The hotel is the obvious place to try the produce, though they have begun to make their way further afield. They include a serene and easy-going **Blonde** (4%), a light and faintly agricultural **IPA** (5%) and a smooth and interesting winter-warming **Bourbon Stout** (5%).

Hogs Head Brew House

1 Stanley Street, Sowerby Bridge, HX6 2AH; T: 01422 836585;
W: thehogsheadbrewhouse.com; E: hogsheadbrewpub@outlook.com;
🅕 🅘 @hogsheadbrewhouse

A recent expansion at this 18th-century former malthouse has secured its place as the biggest brewery in Calderdale – if you temporarily overlook the behemoth that is Vocation.

Even so, with brewing only taking place once a week almost all the produce is sold on the premises, with just the odd cask making its way to local beer festivals. Building work is under way to expand capacity still further by annexing a neighbouring building, which should also increase the quantity sold in cans to local farmers' markets and through a web shop, allowing these beers to be enjoyed further afield.

Its handsome copper and stainless steel brewing vats – some of which are still in use – are an attractive feature of the impressive Hogs Head bar, whose 6,500 square feet are spread over two floors and a covered beer garden. "During Covid-19 we actually held back on developing the brewery and concentrated on adapting the pub," says brewer Mike Stocks. "We developed our outside space with a tent and outdoor heaters and plenty of socially-distanced seating. Inside we finished developing our

second floor to allow more people to visit whilst still feeling safe."

Six of the eight handpumps and several of the keg lines are dedicated to showing off the Hogs Head beers. They include **White Hog** (4%), a lightly-flavoured golden session ale with a mellow citrus aroma and taste, and amber best bitter **Hoppy Valley** (4.3%), full-bodied maltloaf followed by a dry fruity aftertaste. **6 to 8 Weeks** (4%) is a traditional Yorkshire bitter, **Hogsläger** (4.7%) a clean-tasting pils, while there's a perilously easy-drinking nature to the rich raisin and roast malt porter **Old Schnozzler** (5.2%).

Further diversions can be made by way of various specials – like the devilish chocolate and chilli stout **Habanero Hog** (5.5%), uber-hoppy New England pale ale **Hop Rocket** (4.1%), smoked honey porter **Bees Knees** (4.2%) and the Belgian-influenced witbier **Hazy Days** (5.5%) brewed with orange, coriander and cumin.

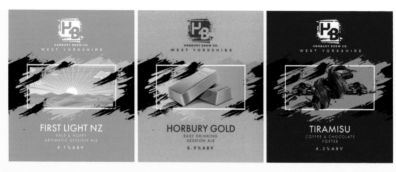

Horbury Ales

Brewers Pride, Low Mill Road, Ossett, WF5 8ND; T: 07970 299292;
E: jon@horburyales.co.uk; 🅵 🅓 *@horburyales*

Founded on a one-barrel plant in 2016, Horbury decamped to a larger plant at the Brewer's Pride in Ossett, though Horbury's Cherry Tree Inn remains the brewery tap.

The 2019 edition of this book remarked on the brewery's minimalist pump clips, but a serious makeover has created a series of designs every bit as impressive as the beers. I'd previously described their New Zealand pale **First Light** (4.1%) as "sunshiney" and perhaps that also influenced the golden dawn scene which now adorns the pumps.

Others in a core range which never gets above five per cent ABV include the sessionable, moderately hopped **Horbury Gold** (3.9%), the Cherry Tree's biggest seller, and the indulgent coffee and chocolate porter **Tiramisu** (4.3%). **Citra** (4.3%) and **Ernest** (3.9%) are among a series of single-hopped ales.

Horsforth Brewery

143 New Rd Side, Horsforth, Leeds, LS18 4JZ; T: 07854 078330;
W: horsforthbrewery.co.uk; E: info@horsforthbrewery.co.uk;
🅯 🅾 🅞 *@horsforthbrewer*

Mark Costello juggled his regular job at the Yorkshire Building Society with being the force majeure at Horsforth Brewery, initially producing his beers in a domestic garage before moving into new premises late in 2018. By the time Horsforth reached its new home in 2020, Mark was full-time.

But the move brought unexpected consequences: "We ordered a new brewkit – but when I saw the cost of installing it, I thought 'I'll do it mi'sen'. We were basically doing it all day, carrying in fermenters and brewing vessels, and I completely knackered my shoulder." So the daily manual labour of the brewing process is now beyond him: "Every time I give it a go, my shoulder goes again."

So when I called in at their beer festival over the 2023 Easter weekend, the five-barrel kit was being operated by former Meanwood brewer Joe Robshaw – though his imminent move to the north-east meant Mark was recruiting a replacement: "It's important to bring in people that are better than you, who will improve the brewery," he says.

The range of beers has certainly been shaken up of late. The hazy, tropical fruit **Horsforth Pale** (4.5%) has now been renamed **Trinity** (4.2%). "Our customers loved it but bars didn't buy it," says Mark. The rebrand and the reduction of strength has worked wonders: "It's selling like hot cakes now."

Originally created for a local mexican restaurant, **El Calavera** ('The Skull') (4%) is a crisp hybrid lime pale, lagered for two weeks, and now a big seller. **By The Hair Of Ernie** (5.4%) is a double dry-hopped kveik,

 Enjoy The Journey (7.2%)
This sweetish, resinous, dry-hopped West Coast IPA is Mark's homage to Sierra Nevada's phenomenal Torpedo. It's a cracker too, and, rather dangerously, tastes nothing like its formidable strength. "This is my contribution to our Icons series," says Mark. "I want everyone in the brewery to brew their own beer." Brewer Joe's contribution is the fulsome **Nightcrawler** stout (5%).

Mark Costello

and the product of a hangover. "I didn't really know what I was doing, and just had to come up with a beer," said Mark. Ernie, of course, is his dog. **Brew Order** (4.5%) is a nicely balanced dry pale, **Rubis** (6.2%) a raspberry saison.

Local pubs and cricket clubs are the main places to find these beers, as well as at the brewery's own attractive taproom which is open every day except Monday; Tuesday is cinema night.

"The last three years have been incredibly hard, but the last six months have been a lot better," says Mark. "We have got some momentum now. You still have to work hard, but now we're getting the results."

HQ Brew

The Harlequin, 108 Nursery Street, Sheffield, S3 8GG; T: 07794 156916; W: www.hqbrew.uk; E: harley@hqbrew.uk

This popular pub on the north side of Sheffield City Centre was essentially the tap for Exit 33 brewing, which was another of the many which closed down for good during the pandemic. Undeterred, long-serving licensee Liz Aspden launched a crowdfunding appeal to establish HQ Brew as a social enterprise, with all profits donated to charities and organisations supporting women and girls – predominantly in South Yorkshire.

Ice Cream Factory

21 Fetter Lane, York, YO1 6EH; W: theicecreamfactory.com; E: mike@theicecreamfactory.co.uk; T: 07880 547393

Sessionable American-influenced **Social Pale** (4%) is an addition to the roster at this new microbrewery established in the former Capaldi's ice cream factory in the centre of York after a period spent brewing with Jolly Sailor in Selby. Hazy pale ales **Volume 1** (6%) and **Spacecraft** (6%) were their early interpretations of the IPA style.

Ilkley Brewery

Ashlands Road, Ilkley, LS29 8JT; T: 01943 604604; W: ilkleybrewery.co.uk;
E: maryjane@ilkleybrewery.co.uk; 🄵 🄳 🄾 *@ilkleybrewery*

"In the context of the world we live in, and the changes we are facing, I'm pleased with the way things are going," says director Luke Raven over a morning coffee in his office in Ilkley Brewery, close to the River Wharfe.

The challenges of the past four years have not just disrupted a business model primed for consistent growth, but have made them re-examine their ethos and their whole reason to be.

"Covid turned off all the taps at once," says Luke. "I really felt for the breweries which didn't have relationships with the supermarkets. We managed to build and launch a direct delivery website in a week, just before lockdown – and moved into a new way of working."

But even when lockdowns ended, pubs re-opened and business began to get back to normal, Ilkley had to face down a second shock. "Our biggest export market was Russia. We were sending eight or nine pallets a month – about 80% of our exports. We had more permanent lines in Moscow than in Leeds."

Russia's invasion of Ukraine ended that trade almost overnight. A shipment which was ready to go just before the invasion was kept back

for a two-day fundraiser on the site, raising money for Ukrainian refugee groups. It was almost emblematic of a brewery which has turned its primary focus to its own backyard: "Local is key to us now," says Luke. "We want to support the pubs that supported us through difficult times."

So Ilkley has cut down on the number of wholesalers it was using to take beer nationwide, while its exports have been trimmed down to their much smaller markets of Italy and Scandinavia. And by placing greater emphasis on its relationships with pubs and with the customers using their web shop, the brewery now has greater control over its business.

"We're becoming a lot more grounded," says Luke. "Some people might call it 'downsizing' but we call it right-sizing."

The brewery's long-term success is founded on the enduring pleasures of the excellent **Mary Jane** (3.5%) which takes its name from one of the protagonists of famous folk song Ilkley Moor Baht'at. The song recounts the tale of the fair Mary Jane who goes courting on Ilkley Moor with a chap who has an ill-advised and ultimately fatal lack of headwear. This much-loved session bitter has some fruitiness to the aroma – lemon, peach and floral notes – but the taste is crisp, cool, refreshing, almost lager-like, and it delivers a long bitter aftertaste.

Mary's alcohol-free cousin **Maiden Mary** is now Ilkley's second biggest seller, and alongside **Nowt Mary** coffee stout, forms a pair of zero-percent beers as good as you'll find anywhere. "Nowt Mary has absolutely flown out since its release earlier last year," says Luke. "It really has defied expectations, and been the source of 90% of our customer feedback over the past few months, with many drinkers who profess not to like dark beer actually loving this!"

Others in the core range include the New World-influenced **Ilkley Pale** (4.2%), the honey and mandarin-accented **Ilkley Blonde** (3.9%) and cheeky Tetley tribute **Joshua Jane** (3.7%). Local restaurants do a good trade in kegged Mary Jane and the crunchy-crisp lager **Slake** (4.5%).

But the range changes all the time as Ilkley produces at least one new beer every month, including some in its Tribus Range, which each harness a different combination of three hops.

Yet amid this plethora of wonderful beers, Luke remains mindful of the economic challenges facing the industry. "The cost of malt has gone up by 40%, hops by 20%, and our energy costs are rising all the time. And we are simply having to swallow these production cost increases because we just can't pass them on to our customers. So we're really investing in efficiency to increase the yield from the brewing process."

And having made the long retreat from Moscow, Luke's ambitions are much more focused on local trade: "We want to be recognised as one of the top cask producers in the region," he says. They're well on the way.

🍺 **Alpha Beta** (4.5%)

There's a big tropical fruit aroma and full-on peach, mango and grapefruit taste to this bright and golden gluten-free session ale, which gives the lie to any suggestion that an IPA needs strength to generate genuine flavour and character. From its first bite to its long and satsifying finish, Alpha Beta hits all the right buttons. "For me, it's the tastiest beer that we do," says Luke. "In terms of flavour you get an amazing bang for your buck."

Imperial Club Brewery

Arcadia Hall, Cliff Street, Mexborough, S64 9HU; T: 01709 584000;
🅵 *@impbrewery*

The lively Imperial
Club just outside the
centre of Mexborough
is the tap for this
micro-brewery and
well worth a visit. It's
a simple, wide-open
beer hall with a stage
at one end and a bar
at the other; an array
of musical instruments
hang from the ceiling
while vintage rock
posters jostle for space
with pump clips above
the bar. Alongside

three guest ales, four of the Imperial brews were available on my visit.
For me, the best was the dark, smooth and slightly treacly, traditional
Yorkshire ale **Classical Bitter** (3.9%). There are some admirable
warming, mellow, fruity notes to the blonde ale **Nah Then** (4.5%), while
the super pale **Platinum Blonde** (4%) has more of the sharp, refreshing
nature that its colour suggests. New to the core range, west coast
IPA **Golden Gate** (5.5%) blends Columbus, Cascade and Citra hops,
though **Stout Wi Nowt Tekken Out** (6%) remains a high-octane, dark
and dangerous beast.

Iron Rabbit

Leeds; W: ironrabbitbrewery.co.uk; 🅵 *@IronRabbitBrewery;*
🐦 *@ironrabbitbrew*

Though primarily a home-brew operator, rabbit-in-chief Mike Massen took
a first step towards commercial brewing in the company of Quirky Ales.
His smoky porter **The First And The Last** references the nickname of
the Liverpool Pals' regiment – the first to be called up and the last to be
stood down – and honours Mike's great uncle Private Arthur Seanor who

died within 20 minutes of 'going over the top' on the first day of the Somme. Unlike some smoked beers, whose smokiness becomes their defining quality, here there is a subtlety, just a wisp of danger, which pervades a beer whose malty, chocolate and coffee character is equally significant. The beer was released to coincide with the centenary of the armistice, with all proceeds going to the Royal British Legion and is regularly revived each November.

Following his own tastes Mike primarily brews porters using their deep taste as a base note to which he adds coffee, chocolate, and even chilli flake tea to give an extra dimension. Currently only available to family and friends Mike does have plans to grow into a commercial enterprise once retirement hits. "In the meantime, I'm just practising my craft and continuing my search for the perfect porter."

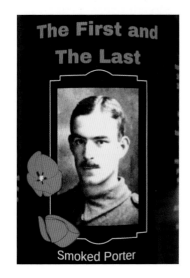

Smoked Porter

Isaac Poad Brewing

The Hay House, Baxby Manor, Husthwaite, North Yorks, YO61 4PW
T: 01423 358114; W: isaacpoadbrewing.co.uk; E: beer@isaacpoad.co.uk;
🛇 @isaacpoadbrewingyork; 🐦 @isaacpoadbeer; 📷 @isaacpoadbrewing

Grain traders for more than a century and a half, Isaac Poad diversified into beer in 2016, building on long-established local connections to source their materials; aside from the hops, everything is grown in Yorkshire.

A re-brand has seen a change of name and design across all their beers. **Session IPA** (4.5%) is a crisp pale whose citric attack steals stealthily across the palate; **Piccadilly** (4.8%) is a deep-tasting chocolate and coffee porter, while deep amber and nutty **Best Bitter** (3.8%) stirs warm memories of high-watermark Tetley Bitter. The floral, citric newcomer **New York** (4.2%) was a winner at the 2022 Great Taste Awards.

John Smith's

The Brewery, Tadcaster, LS24 9SA; T: 01937 832091; W: johnsmiths.co.uk;
E: customerservices@johnsmiths.co.uk; 🅕 *@johnsmithsuk*

The Romans called this area Calcaria – the Latin for lime kilns – reflecting the magnesium limestone which lends the local water a hardness which was critical to the establishment of a vast industry.

Brewing has been a cornerstone of Tadcaster life for over 250 years. Stephen Hartley established the original Tadcaster Brewery in 1758, and it passed through several generations of his and the Backhouse families before the Smiths emerged onto the scene.

The eldest child of a wealthy Leeds businessman, John Smith was a remarkable figure who – if you are prepared to believe the tall tales of the company website – excelled at origami as a child, attended university at 13, and at 18 built a steam-driven helicopter.

Aviation's loss was brewing's gain, and in 1852 Smith bought the Backhouse and Hartley Brewery, soon moving his operation next door and gifting the old brewery to his nephew Samuel Smith.

The brewery grew slowly at first, but following Smith's death in 1879 expanded rapidly, increasing production to service an ever-growing chain of public houses. By the time it became part of the Courage group in 1970, John Smith's owned 1,800 licensed premises across the north; alongside the parent company's vast southern holdings, it became a truly national pub and brewing operation. Hardly surprisingly, the Tadcaster beer soon found favour with southern drinkers.

It is now a global brand, marketed worldwide by Heineken. It's perhaps a shame then, that it scarcely represents the cream of Yorkshire brewing. **John Smith's Original** (3.6%) is an uncomplicated brew of moderate malt and minimal hop character, whose sales were nonetheless massively boosted by the 'No Nonsense' advertising campaigns fronted by comedians Jack Dee and Peter Kay. They garnered the sixth most advertising awards worldwide while sales increased by more than 65%.

Between this and its rather spineless cousin **Extra Smooth** (3.6%) John Smith's now outsells any other ale in the UK. With a capacity of around 3.8 million hectolitres, John Smith's is one of the country's biggest breweries and also produces some of Heineken's international lager brands including **Kronenbourg** (5%) and **Amstel** (4.1%).

Up the road, Sam Smith's continues to plough its own unique furrow.

Jolly Boys' Brewery

Redbrook Business Park, Wilthorpe Lane, Barnsley, South Yorkshire, S75 1JN;
T: 07900 403206; W: jollyboys-brewery.co.uk;
E: h.roberts@jollyboysbrewery.co.uk; 🄵 🄳 *@jollybrewery*

"It's been a turbulent time," says director Hywel Roberts, reflecting on the impact of the pandemic on a brewery which was really beginning to hit its straps before Covid landed. "But we've come through. To paraphrase Tom Waits, our dreams haven't been shattered, they just walk with a limp."

Like many great ideas, the Jolly Boys' Brewery began life over a few pints in a pub. Four friends, all of them educators, realised that a business idea was something they wanted to pursue. "The Jolly Boys have all spent their working lives contributing via their day jobs to the support of others in society," says Hywel. "This moral drive is important to us. Couple this with a love of beer, respect for community and pride in doing a good job, we made a life-changing decision: we were going to brew beer. What more honourable and worthwhile calling could there be?

"If The Jolly Boys' Brewery were a person, they'd be a listener, a carer, a mood-lifter, honest and true. They'd be non-bureaucratic and free-spirited. They'd also get a round in."

Since their first brew in 2016, the Jolly Boys have brewed an eclectic range of predominantly moderate-strength ales including the robust **Jolly Collier Porter** (5%), the pale **Jolly YPA** (4.8%) and **Jolly Blonde** (4%). Recent additions include the light and hazy American-influenced **Supa-Citra** (4.2%).

While their Real Ale Café has now closed, plans are afoot for both a station bar and a new city-centre venue.

Jolly Sailor Brewery

77 Barlby Road, Selby, YO8 5AB; T: 01757 707564; W: jollysailorbrewery.uk;
E: jollysailorbrewery@gmail.com; 🇫 *@jollysailorbrewery;* 🇽 📷 *@jollysailorbrew*

A thriving web shop and a healthy trade in beer boxes saw the brewery glide confidently through the pandemic like an old sailor riding out a hurricane.

Though named after the excellent Jolly Sailor pub in Cawood, the brewery itself is five miles away in an old boxing club behind the Olympia Hotel on the outskirts of Selby. Both pubs stock the beers, and the brewery's tenth anniversary in 2022 was celebrated with both a new sessionable hazy pale ale **Decade** (4.5%) and the launch of a new ship's wheel logo.

I first encountered the convivial transatlantic **Selby Pale** (3.9%) during a visit to the Olympia. Its character shaped by the powerful influence of Nugget and Cascade hops from the US and the Maris Otter and Munich Malts from the UK, there's a slight tart tang when it first crosses the lips but the freshness of mangoes and a spicy, herby complexity is nailed to a solid malty base.

While changing specials freshens up the range, core products include the amber, biscuity **Selby Bitter** (3.8%), jet-black and treacly **Selby Mild** (4%) and the smooth coffee and chocolate porter **Dark Nights** (5%).

Selby Blonde (3.8%)
A couple of bottles of this offered welcome comfort as I worked on this book during one of the lazy, balmy days of the 2022 August heatwave. Slightly hazy, this fresh-tasting beer is as soft as feathers, light and delightfully easy-going. Perhaps some extra cooling would add further bite and crispness, but on this warm day it proved a deliciously convivial companion, and just what I needed.

Junction Brewpub

1 Baildon Rd, Baildon, BD17 6AB; T: 01274 582009;
🐦 *@Junctionbaildonofficial*

The curious shape of the Junction freehouse is a product of its location. It sits at a busy narrow fork in the road; turning left the road climbs steeply towards the centre of Baildon, going right the flatter main road heads for Otley. Doubtless the architect had to think hard to design something to suit these challenging co-ordinates.

For drinkers who like to choose on the basis of colour, the Junction's names offer an easy guide. Brewed primarily for the pub, they include significantly-hopped **Blonde** (4%), sweetish porter **Dark Thoughts** (4.6%) and fruity **Golden Splendour** (3.8%). The choice in the pub changes frequently, and often includes selections from across Bradford and the wider region.

The rescuers – Sheffield venue owner Jim O'Hara, former Kelham Island boss Ed Wickett and Thornbridge Brewery's Simon Webster.

Kelham Island Brewery

23 Alma Street, Sheffield, S3 8SA; T: 0114 249 4804;
W: kelhambrewery.co.uk; E: sales@kelhambrewery.co.uk;
🅵 🆇 *@kelhambrewery;* 🆘 *@kelham_island_brewery*

Amid almost three years of bad news – great pubs closing, breweries struggling, livelihoods under threat – the closure of Kelham Island Brewery seemed the unkindest cut of all.

When academic Dave Wickett founded Kelham Island in the beer garden of Sheffield's Fat Cat pub in 1990 it was a speculative venture at a time when – despite CAMRA's undoubted progress – cask beer remained at the margins of drinking culture. It was the city's first new independent brewery in almost a century, and in time came to be recognised as one of a handful of pioneering outliers who laid the groundwork for Britain's beer revolution.

Much of its success was founded on **Pale Rider** (5.2%), a big tasting, slightly sweet and popcorn-accented pale golden ale which was on the roster from the early days and soon became the brewery's most famous name and biggest seller. Even as the craft ale scene blossomed, Kelham Island held its own amid stiff competition, particularly from some big-hitting newcomers to its own neighbourhood. After his death in 2012, Dave remained revered as one of its founding fathers; his son Ed led the business for the decade that followed.

So the brewery's closure in 2022 came as a hammer blow, and particularly to Sheffield, in the same way that Leeds Brewery's closure was such a shock 30 miles further north. If giants like these can fall, what hope for the rest?

But for Kelham Island, this was not the end of the road, as a consortium of local businesspeople got together to ensure its survival. Among them is Simon Webster of Derbyshire's Thornbridge Brewery, who said: "Kelham Island Brewery was the reason we started Thornbridge and Dave Wickett was a guiding hand in our early days. When I first heard about the closure, I immediately thought about how we could help."

Ed Wickett added: "I'm really pleased the brewery is in such safe hands. It'll be great to serve Pale Rider in the Fat Cat again."

Kibble Brewery *New*

The Crystal Palace, 11 Towngate, Thurlstone, Sheffield, S36 9RH; T: 01226 766331

Named after a huge bucket used to hoist materials from pit shafts, this newcomer namechecks mining traditions; the pump clip's pithead winding gear and beers such as the crisp **Kent Thin Pale Ale** (4.2%) and the dark stone-fruit **Barnsley Bed Bitter** (4.2%) further emphasise coal's heritage. The brewery was established in the car park of Thurlstone's Crystal Palace pub which remains the best place to try the wares; some of the kit was salvaged from the former Hamelsworde brewery, a few miles east of here.

Kirkstall Brewery

100 Kirkstall Road, Leeds, LS3 1JA; T: 0113 898 0280;
W: kirkstallbrewerycompany.com; E: info@kirkstallbrewery.com;
🖪 ⊚ @kirkstallbrewery; 𝕏 @kirkstallbrew

Few places can claim so long a history of brewing. The Cistercian monks of Kirkstall Abbey started making beer here over 800 years ago and perhaps still would be, had it not been for the disastrous intervention of a King hell-bent on a split with Rome.

Some 300 years after the dissolution, the tradition was revived in Georgian times by the first Kirkstall Brewery who unloaded their barrels directly onto barges on the Leeds-Liverpool canal which passed right behind the brewhouse and gave Kirkstall a ready means of transport to Lancashire and beyond.

For 150 years, they were a big player on the local scene, before they were closed down by giant owners Whitbread in 1983. The original stone-built tower brewery, complete with its chimney, is now home to up to 1,000 students, many of whom will no doubt have made acquaintance with beers from the new brewery which opened nearby in 2011, before relocating to much larger premises in a former dairy in Kirkstall Road in 2016. They are now the city's biggest brewer – a point underlined by the closure of heavyweight local rival Leeds Brewery late in 2022, a blow significantly softened by their great beers now being welcomed into the Kirkstall fold.

Kirkstall's success is founded on a core range of three great ales. Fragrant, hoppy **Kirkstall Pale** (4%) has become one of the ubiquitous beers on Leeds city-centre bars, while the more potent **Three Swords** (4.5%) is a clean-tasting pale ale with some suggestions of lemon and lime. Full-bodied **Black Band Porter** (5.5%) is a smooth and red black ale with a hearty fireside blend of milky coffee and dark fruits.

"The pandemic kicked us up the arse," admits Kirkstall managing director John Kelly, over a pint in the Cardigan Arms, the Victorian jewel in his growing portfolio of pubs. "We didn't have an online shop or a decent web presence." Taking a crash course in web-design allowed John to address this, while accelerating the installation of a canning line enabled Kirkstall to stay in the game. Production was concentrated onto canned beers such as crisp and sharp West Coast IPA **Spokane** (6%), grassy,

106

grapefruity New England Pale **Providence** (5.2%), and **Verdita** (4%) with its complex character of lime, pineapple, mint and coriander.

In bottle, the perfect pale, modestly carbonated and deeply bitter **Dissolution** (5%) is a dangerously easy-drinking IPA which takes its name from Henry VIII's ruinous sacking of the established church, which reduced the local abbey to a stone shell – albeit one which now plays host to the wonderful Leeds International Beer Festival. Thankfully Kirkstall's own on-site taproom didn't go the same way: "It only opened three weeks before lockdown," says John. "It became a graveyard where non-furloughed staff lingered as ghosts during the pandemic, and we all got to know far too much about each other!"

Now through the hiatus, demand continues to grow, exemplified by the installation of two new tanks which have added 200,000 pints to capacity. And John sees plenty of reasons for optimism: "We're facing intense pressures, but the right operators will thrive."

The arrival of brewer Stuart Ross, formerly of Magic Rock, has catalysed Kirkstall's new Prize Ales series, each based on a historic recipe. East Kent Golding hops lend some forest fruit notes to the gentle old-style **Bitter** (3.8%), while a greater bill of malt and hops concentrates these flavours into the more full-bodied **Extra Bitter** (4.4%).

There is some chocolate and coffee cake sweetness to the deceptively potent **XXX Mild** (6.5%), while the autumnal **Biscuit Brown** (4.5%) derives deep crunchy biscuit flavour from malts and oats baked in the Kirkstall taproom's pizza oven. A world away from the uber-hopped versions of today, **AK IPA** (5%) is a soft, refreshing yeasty ale based on a Victorian Kirkstall recipe. As this book went to press Kirkstall was

planning The Great Exhibition, a festival featuring traditional and re-discovered old ales from breweries across the region.

As for the future: "It's all about more pubs," says John. The Crown at Addingham is the latest addition to a portfolio which already includes the Sparrow in Bradford, the elegant nine-bedroomed Black Horse in Otley – as well as the taproom, the Cardy and the nearby Kirkstall Bridge, a serial winner of Leeds CAMRA's pub of the year prize. "The demand for good beer will always be there; great pubs will continue to flourish," he says.

That brewery founder Steve Holt is an obsessive collector of breweriana enables Kirkstall to pack their pubs with old-style taproom character, as well as great beers.

 Virtuous (4.5%)

When first launched in 2018, Virtuous was intentionally marketed as an alternative to the mass market beers such as Cobra and Kingfisher which are the tried-and-tested choices of many an Indian restaurant. Yet since those first pints were poured at the Aagrah restaurant in Leeds city centre, this clean and generously-hopped, gluten-free session IPA has become a phenomenon to eclipse virtually all the others on the Kirkstall roster. Rather like Ilkley's wonderful Alpha Beta, this beer of moderate strength is chock-a-block with taste and character – and has become a fragrant, grapefruity, lemon-and-lime presence right across the city and far beyond. Re-packaging it in yellow and blue as **We All Love Leeds**, found a thirsty new audience among football fans as Kirkstall moved quickly into canning when fears of a lockdown turned into reality. And now, Virtuous has become the go-to choice in pubs, curry houses, supermarkets and more. "It continues to astound us," says John Kelly.

Lady Luck Brewery

The Little Angel, 18 Flowergate, Whitby,
YO21 3BA; T: 01947 820475;
f *@ladyluckbrewerywhitby*

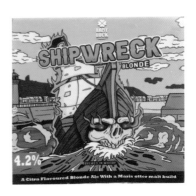

A Citra Flavoured Blonde Ale With a Maris otter malt build

Early in 2023, a visit to this lively naval-themed pub of low ceilings, stained glass and polished wood, close to the harbour and popular with the visiting Goths, offered a perfect opportunity to sample the Lady Luck range.

The bright translucent blonde ale **Shipwreck** (4.2%) is a juicy pale with some nice mandarin notes, while golden and refreshing **Pirate's Treasure** (4%) has a hoppy suggestion of grapefruit.

Firmer and more assertive is the jet-black **Space Dinosaurs Love Chocolate** (5%), where cacao nibs and cocoa powder lend their weight to a beer of chocolate and burnt toffee richness. Its only missed step is the greengrocer's apostrophe on the pump clip.

Triple Chocolate Stout Flavoured With Cocoa Powder , Cacao Nibs and Chocolate malt

Bitter Bite (4.5%)
Despite the fearsome burger-munching shark on the pump clip, this is a very easy-going creature. It's an old-style traditional bitter, a bright copper colour with a tight creamy head and the gentle bitterness of Bramling Cross hops balanced by some soothing malt. It's a great example of a Yorkshire cask ale – and it's brewed on the premises.

Lamb Brewing *New*

Queen's Arms, Litton, Skipton, BD23 5QJ; T: 07900 013245;
E: hello@lambbrewing.com; 🄵 🄾 *@lambbrewing*

Like at the Fox and Newt in Burley, brewing at the Queen's Arms in Litton, north of Skipton, has been sporadic over the years. Previous incumbent Littondale took over here in 2017 but sadly closed during the pandemic.

Now local brewer Thomas Crapper has revived the operation as Lamb Brewing, focused on quality, cask-conditioned ales brewed to determinedly traditional British recipes at the kind of sessionable strengths which make them perfect refreshers after a day's walking or cycling amid the dramatic scenery nearby.

They include the golden, light and easy-going **Pale** (3.9%), the modestly sweet and spicy **Bitter** (3.7%) and both a light and dark version of the gently refreshing **X Mild** (3.2%).

The old-style pump clips emphasise the sense that this is very much a vintage drinking experience; the Queen's Arms is the ideal setting to try these beers as fresh and perfect as can be.

Back in business – Leeds Brewery's Rob Warriner flanked by Kirkstall Brewery's Managing Director John Kelly, left, and owner Steve Holt.

Leeds Brewery

100 Kirkstall Road, Leeds, LS3 1JA; T: 0113 898 0280; W: leedsbrewery.co.uk; 🅵 🅓 *@theleedsbrewery;* 🅞 *@leedsbrewery*

The closure of Leeds Brewery in late 2022 came as a huge shock, particularly to those who had loved their beers over the past 15 years or so. Just before Christmas, news emerged that the beers were to be preserved across town at Kirkstall Brewery – allowing drinkers to continue to experience the significant pleasures of classic Yorkshire Bitter **Leeds Best** (4.3%), crisp and refreshing **Leeds Pale** (3.8%) and the full bodied dark ale **Midnight Bell** (4.8%).

"It was their life and they tried to keep it alive," says head brewer Rob Warriner, looking back at how long-standing business partners Sam Moss and Michael Brothwell threw everything into fighting the winding-up petition which ultimately led to the closure of their Beeston brewery.

But a big local rival soon rode to the rescue: "If anyone was going to do it, it was us," says

John Kelly, managing director at Kirkstall Brewery. "We've known the guys from Leeds for ages."

"It's always been friendly competition," says Rob. "Kirkstall's plans ensured that the brand would survive."

There was no interruption to production, and Rob's first brew on the Kirkstall kit, using Leeds's recipes and own unique yeast strain, was immediate vindication for the move. "It sparkled in the glass; it absolutely WAS Leeds Pale."

The other Leeds beers have also been given a new lease of life in LS3: the crisp, clean and dry continental lager **Leodis** (4.6%), light but firmly bitter **Yorkshire Gold** (4%) and the satisfying mainstream IPA **Monsoon** (4%). "The best thing about Leeds Brewery has always been that we made beer that we liked for pubs that we like – and I can stick by that mantra at Kirkstall," says Rob.

And just as the brewery's Leeds pubs were long ago sold to Cameron's – yet continued to stock the full range – I suspect many drinkers will fail to realise that anything has changed.

Leeds Co-Hoperative

W: leedshops.co.uk; E: leedshops@gmail.com; 🎧 🔘 *@leedshops*

I'm not sure if the sinister hand of climate change can be felt in this development, but hops – once the preserve of England's southern counties – are now being grown in Leeds, 200 miles north of the heartlands of Kent and Sussex, Worcs and Warks.

Each year, members of the Co-Hoperative group cultivate hop plants in their gardens and on allotments, before harvesting the chunky green flowers to create a new beer. "We started with Cascade, but a lot of members now grow the dwarf hop Prima Donna – it's a bit easier to manage if you only have a small garden," says Sharon Scarmazzo, who each year co-ordinates the growing, the collecting, the brewing – and the drinking!

Sharon, who was bitten by the craft beer bug while living in San Francisco, has been involved in the group almost from the start: "It was my opportunity to

Sharon Scarmazzo

Members of the Leeds Co-Hoperative trying the fruits of their labours at the Kirkstall Brewery tap

put my enthusiasm into action."

It's October 2022 and we're talking in the Kirkstall Brewery tap as the group cracks the cask on their latest brew, named **Vespers** (4.5%) to honour connections to the nearby abbey. "We use green hops, not dried or pelleted or put through any kind of process, so these have to be used within 24 hours of being picked." Though the results are different every time, this year's brew proves light, fresh, golden, slightly earthy and packed with juicy grapefruit.

After a false start in 2017 when technical hitches ruined the beer, for four years Nomadic handled the brewing, first at the Fox and Newt pub in Burley and then at their own brewhouse in Sheepscar. Their sad demise saw Kirkstall step into the breach.

"We collected around 36 kilograms of hops this time round," says Sharon. "That's allowed us to brew 26 barrels, and these will be on sale in pubs around Leeds."

Well, that's once the hop-growers had finished their own celebration, wiping out the first cask-and-a half on launch night: "It's just a nice group of people who get together and talk about all things beer. And it's a lot of fun."

Legitimate Industries

10 Weaver Street, Leeds, LS4 2AU; W: legitimateworldwide.com;
🖪 *@legitimateindustries;* 🖸 *@Legitimate Ind*

Based around the concept of a rapacious multi-national, Legitimate Industries' marketing strategy has given us beers with names like **Timeshare Scam** and **Double Agent**. Their website features a rogues' gallery of company directors – and unsavoury host of spivs, escorts and drugs suspects – and tells how the brewkit was asset-stripped from an ailing rival.

For Legitimate Industries' faux-criminal hype to work, it has to be built around quality. Hazy yellow **Identity Theft** (5.3%) delivers bags of substance – a significant dry pale ale which is packed with kiwi and grapefruit and a long aftertaste which slowly builds the warmth you might expect of a beer of this premium strength.

Despite their claims to having offices "from Pyongyang to Panama" even the contact details offer no clue of their real whereabouts, though the legal requirement to include an address on the cans nails them to a rather more prosaic address in inner-city Leeds. The merchandise includes session IPA **Election Fraud** (4%) which has some legitimate mango and orange, and the crisp, surprisingly floral pilsner **Tax Evasion** (4.4%).

Little Critters Brewery

Unit 5, Neepsend Industrial Estate, 80 Parkwood Rd, Sheffield, S3 8AG;
T: 0114 2763171; W: littlecrittersbrewery.com; E: info@littlecrittersbrewery.com;
🖪 *@smallbatchbeers;* 🖸 *@littlecritsbrew;* 🖸 *@littlecrittersbrewery*

Barely fledglings when the first edition of this book was published, Little Critters continue to add new species of beer to their colourful menagerie. This family-run microbrewery produces just 2,000 cans in each batch, decorating each with wacky and wonderful artwork.

Their growing flock now includes the imaginatively-titled English pale ale **Malty Python** (4.8%), and the smooth and powerful espresso stout **King Crow** (7.2%), which delicately blends silky chocolate with the dark bitterness of roasted coffee beans.

Chocolate and crystal malts combine with bittersweet orange peel in the dark **Orange Utan** (5%) chocolate stout, while **Nutty Ambassador** (6%) is a smooth and luxurious hazelnut milk stout. **Macaw Blimey** (7.7%) is a potent double IPA, powered by a blend of South America's El Dorado hop with Citra and Mosaic.

Great Danish (7.4%)

This super strong maple and pecan pastry stout develops Orange Utan's chocolate theme still further, adding pecan extract and maple syrup to create a sweet and treacly cocktail. This rich, luxurious melange of flavours almost feels like a bizarre wintry one-off, a gag to share among friends. It's no session beer and unlikely to appeal to lovers of a traditional stout – but as an occasional delicious treat, it's rather wonderful.

Little Mesters Brewing

352 Meadowhead, Sheffield, S8 7UJ; W: littlemestersbrewing.co.uk;
E: info@littlemestersbrewing.co.uk; ⓕ *@littlemestersbrewing;*
ⓧ *@LMBrewing;* ⓘ *@little_mesters_brewing*

The original Little Mesters were a key cog in Sheffield's world-renowned cutlery and toolmaking machine. A network of highly-skilled, self-employed craftspeople, working from small workshops or their own

homes, each Little Mester concentrated on an individual aspect of the process – forging, grinding or finishing – and many specialised on particular products such as razors, cutlery, penknives or surgical instruments.

This new brewery takes over where Mitchells Hop House left off, moving in when the long-established wine, beer and cigar store closed down its own short-lived brewing operation. **Original Lager** (4%) is a subtly lemony gluten-free pilsner, **Original Pale** (4.5%) a more assertive refresher.

Stan (4.1%) is a special IPA brewed in memory of Stan Shaw, the last little mester, who died in 2021, aged 94. **Original Bitter** (3.9%) is the kind of modestly hopped, nicely malty, fiercely traditional ale that the Mesters would surely have enjoyed after a long day's steely graft.

Little Valley Brewery

Turkey Lodge, New Road, Hebden Bridge, HX7 5TT; T: 01422 883 888;
W: littlevalleybrewery.co.uk; E: info@littlevalleybrewery.co.uk;
ⓕ ⓘ *@littlevalleybrewery;* ⓧ *@littlevalleyale*

Don't be fooled by the name. Little Valley is perched high above Hebden Bridge, and on the afternoon early in 2023 when I made the winding journey up from the valley floor, the hilltop brewery was lashed by high winds and driving rain, the narrow road perilously awash.

I suspect weather conditions were rather different when beer-loving Dutchman Wim van der Spek met partner Sue Cooper. They were both cycling in Nepal – he was pedalling one way and she the other – but after synchronising directions, the couple moved to Yorkshire in 2001 and began peddling beers instead. Here their devotion to great ale

and concern for the planet go hand-in-hand with producing some of the county's best-loved beers, which between them have garnered an impressive collection of awards.

Several honour Pennine placenames. There's moderately flowery and marmalady **Cragg Bitter** (4.2%), spicy, pithy, hazy **Hebden's Wheat** (4.5%) – twice a silver medal winner at the Great British Beer Festival – and the straw-coloured and floral flagship ale **Withens Pale** (3.9%) which takes its name from the windswept fell which reputedly inspired Emily Brontë. Its agreeable nature is perhaps more Cathy than Heathcliff.

Namechecking a local memorial to the Napoleonic Wars, **Stoodley Stout** (4.8%) stretches the envelope in terms of what fullness of flavour might be wrought from a dark beer of under 5%. Its languid, oily pour offers clues to its richness, and it forms an exuberant foaming head, from which enticing dark chocolate aromas emerge. These wash across the palate, where they're joined by plums, chocolate, a whiff of woodsmoke and the dangerous bitter nature of an espresso distilled to rocket-fuel strength.

There's a suggestion of white wine to the understated aroma of the anaemically-pale **Stage Winner** (3.5%) which has so exuberant a white head it might easily be mistaken for a specialist Belgian lager. It celebrates the life of Yorkshire cyclist Brian Robinson – the first Brit ever to win a Tour de France stage. The old-school, well-hopped and slightly grassy **Python IPA** (6%) was drunk by Palin, Cleese et al. during their reunion gigs in 2014. Complex **Tod's Blonde** (5%) is crisp and firmly bitter.

Bright ginger beer **Radical Roots** (4%) pours a bright gold with an

Sue and Wim

extravagant foaming white head from which some gingery notes emerge, and some of that rootsy character continues into the taste where it's backed by bags of firm bitterness, and a lovely dry aftertaste.

At the top of the Little Valley range is the bottle-conditioned organic barley wine **LVBX** (10%). Prising off the cap releases peaty and malty aromas; pouring it reveals its deep red-brown colour. If you hadn't read the label you might easily imagine this a sessionable brown ale or a mid-strength ruby porter, but those illusions are blown away when its whisky-like characteristics treat the palate to a complex blend of bitter woodsmoke and sweet damsons. There are toasty caramel notes in there, but the iron-like firmness and sheer strength of this beer ensures that it quickly begins to work a soporific alchemy on the senses, its powerful influence remaining into a long liqueur coffee aftertaste. Sue tells me that this phenomenal beer isn't currently available; hopefully this will serve as a nudge to bring it back.

 Dark Vale (4.5%)

Wim proffered a couple of bottles of this lovely vanilla porter before I headed back down the valley to Hebden. Characteristically for Little Valley, it packs plenty into a beer of only moderate strength. An aroma of caramel toffee escapes the foaming ivory head before the palate is hit by mellow dark fruits, tobacco and just a suggestion of treacle.

Lords Brewing

Unit 15, Heath House Mill, Golcar, Huddersfield, HD7 4JW; T: 01484 651230;
W: lordsbrewing.com; E: sales@lordsbrewing.com; 🔲 🔲 🔲 *@lordsbrewing*

Golcar Brewery owner John Broadbent inspired three brothers-in-law to establish Lords in 2015, initially using his own spare capacity but now using kit of their own.

There are bags of tropical fruit aromas to the soft and easy-going **Malamute** (4.5%), and these are echoed in the ultra pale, slightly grainy **Silver Spur** (4.6%). **Chosen Man** (4.4%) adds the freshness of New World hops to a classic bitter recipe while **Expedition** is a gently satisfying blonde, **Bandon Car** (4.8%) a roasty porter. Beyond this core range there's an ever-changing menu of specials, craft and hazy ales and bottled beers. An on-site taproom opens up this range to drinkers on the first Friday of each month.

Lost Industry Brewing

Nutwood Trading Estate, Limestone Cottage Lane, Sheffield, S6 1NJ;
T: 07710 793253; E: beer@lostindustrybrewing.com;
🔲 *@lostindustrybrewing;* 🔲 *@lost_industry*

Founded in 2015, this family-run brewery's industrious attitude has forged a reputation for their interesting and progressive expressions of both traditional and contemporary beers. Not having a regular brew has freed them to venture into wheat beers, sours, saisons, Belgian pales and dark ales – as well as the more familiar South Yorkshire territories of bitters, stouts, porters and pales.

A switch towards canning, and selling to bottle shops, helped Lost Industry weather the pandemic. "But times are tough, and a few of our customers have gone under," admits boss Lesley Seaton. "The cost of brewing makes everything difficult as electricity and ingredient prices have increased significantly, and we're no longer able to export thanks to Brexit."

Even so, a determination to survive is exemplified by the new rich coffee stout **Perklife** (5.4%), the sour and fruity cask pale ale **Havana Gang Brawl** (5.7%) and plans for a collaboration with Steel City to create an imperial version of **Lemoncake**. "As usual we're doing a wide range of brews from the traditional to the outrageously experimental – and we're also hoping to do some more barrel ageing later this year.

"We keep hoping that the scene and economy will improve. Only time will tell."

Loxley Brewery

Wisewood Inn, 539 Loxley Road, Sheffield, S6 6RR; T: 0114 233 4310;
W: loxleybrewery.co.uk; E: info@loxleybrewery.co.uk; 🅕 🅣 🅞 *@loxleybrewery*

The Wisewood Inn passed depressingly through the hands of all manner of pub companies, before being finally established as the brewery tap for Loxley Brewery, established in 2018 in a former garage on the site. The revival of this lovely old inn on the north-western fringes of Sheffield, where the city gives way to the rolling countryside of the Peak District, mirrors that of a brewery which has emerged from the pandemic with an ambitious rebrand and the launch of a host of new beers.

Fresh water from the Loxley spring 70 metres beneath the pub forms the backbone to each of them; the twelve-barrel kit is pure Sheffield steel.

The first Loxley beers showed lamentable lack of imagination, at least in the nomenclature – there were **Wisewood 1** and **Wisewood 7**, and all bases in between. But the rebrand, plus the need to sell the beers beyond their mothership, saw the numbers scrapped in favour of zesty blonde ale **Revill** (4%), the bold five-hop pale ale **Lomas** (4.4%) and the **Black Dog** milk stout (5%).

Each references local tragedies, myths and legends. The sharp and citric IPA **Gunson** (4.8%) namechecks the hapless chief waterways engineer on the night of the city's devastating great flood of 1864; sessionable Pacific pale ale **Fearn** (3.8%) recalls an 18th-century murderer, hung in chains nearby for his crimes. The brewery's raven logo plays to this dark theme.

During the first lockdown, Loxley's core beer range was brewed at reduced capacity; bottle-conditioned ales were sold through social media, local deliveries and shops, while a small amount of cask was

distributed via off-sales at local pubs.

In 2021 they took their first venture into keg beers, and have developed an ever-changing range while American Pale Ale **Corvus** (4.2%) and West Coast IPA **Kasper** (5.5%) saw them spread their wings into canning.

A vintage Citroen bread van has been converted into a portable beer bar, and as lockdown restrictions eased, Loxley edged back towards full capacity. When the brewery took over a second pub, the Palm Tree in Walkley, it was soon re-styled as the Raven.

Meanwhile, the Wisewood goes from strength to strength, providing a quality pub food throughout the week, while gaining a city-wide reputation for Sunday roasts. Its three-day summer beer festival makes use of a spacious beer garden to celebrate the very best of the steel city beer scene.

Luddite Brewery

Calder Vale Hotel, Millfield Road, Wakefield, WF4 5EB; T: 01924 277658;
🅕 *@ludditebrewing*

Given that the Luddites were hell-bent on the destruction of all things industrial, it should be barely surprising that this brewery is one of only a few which don't have a website. Their Facebook page and that of the Calder Vale Hotel which stocks their beers, are the best places to find out the latest news. The six-barrel plant brews around once a week, providing Calder Vale customers with beers like the traditionally easy-going Yorkshire Bitter **1812** (4.4%) and crisp **Belgian Blonde** (4.1%).

Magic Rock Brewing

Willow Park Business Centre, Willow Lane, Huddersfield HD1 5EB;
T: 01484 649823; W: magicrockbrewing.com; E: sales@magicrockbrewing.com;
 @magicrockbrewing

Magic Rock is among a special band of brewers who have transcended humble, locally-based beginnings to become a worldwide craft sensation.

When Rich Burhouse founded the brewery in 2011, the name referenced the family gemstone business, and lent itself to an assortment of beers with a big-top, freak-show theme, like gluten-free **Fantasma** (6.5%) which delivers bags of hop-heavy bitterness, and the assertive gloopy, chocolatey, smoky stout **Dark Arts** (6%) which develops just a suggestion of dandelion and burdock sweetness. Cloudy **Saucery** (3.9%) is very much the flagship beer. It explodes on the palate with such a blast of passion fruit, mango and pine it might easily be a good deal stronger.

The brewery moved to its present site on the north site of Huddersfield in 2015, and a massive buyout by Australian giants Lion early in 2019 saw some serious investment – "mostly in terms of quality and efficiency," says Assistant Brand Manager Andrew Kruze. "Sometimes with craft beer it can be these things that are lacking."

Even so, moving into multi-national ownership changed some drinkers' perception of Magic Rock. At beer festivals which once welcomed this much-loved brand, they were suddenly persona non grata. While Andrew can understand this attitude, he insists the brewery ethos never changed. "We still have a lot of staff who have been with us since the

Designer Rich Norgate

early days and they remain passionate about the brand. They ensured we never lost the Magic Rock culture."

That culture is built around a cluster of great beers. Reddish-brown **Rapture** (4.6%) is among their flagship products. Characteristically for this brewery, its use of prodigious quantities of six varieties of hops generates sharp and slightly angular fruit notes to the aroma and plenty of significant juicy fruit flavour. The moderate strength of floral **Ringmaster** (3.9%) belies a beer of substance and significant fruit flavour – lemon, mango and lime.

Though stronger than many, **Cannonball** (7.4%) is absolutely exemplary of the wonderful resurgence of India Pale Ale; its blend of resinous hops delivers a firm and complex taste, with apricot, grapefruit, peach, passion fruit and pine.

As early adopters of canning, the brewery was well placed to ride out

the pandemic. They brought their webshop in house – and ramped up sales of cans and mini-casks. "We were opening our tap in Holmfirth just as Covid hit," says Andrew. "It was the worst possible timing, but the bar switched to doing local deliveries – and even worked with a nearby bar to offer canned cocktails to local customers!"

And with draught beer no longer viable, Covid also afforded the opportunity for more beer to be switched to barrel ageing. Matured in bourbon casks, the dark, dangerous and delicious **Bearded Lady** (10.5%) is emblematic of the project, a full-blooded assault of dark chocolate and rich black treacle with a determined woodsmoke finish. "With some, the longer you leave them in the cask, the better they taste," says Andrew.

Traditionally, before anyone ever heard the word 'sessionable', mild was an easy-going refreshing beer for the working man. The dark and gently carbonated **Mild Out** (4%) with its malty character and pleasing nut and toffee notes is Magic Rock's first take on this time-honoured style.

The anaemically pale zero-alcohol **Free Ride** celebrates the love of cycling shared by a pair of Riches – owner Burhouse and designer Norgate, the long-time art guru behind Magic Rock's distinctive funky labels. You could easily sink a couple of these light, refreshing, lemon and ginger thirst-quenchers after a hot day in the saddle.

In 2022 Lion decided to invest heavily in US brewer Bell's, and in the process divested themselves of their two British craftsters, Magic Rock and Fourpure, which were in turn taken over by a consortium of investors. Their recent re-admission to independent brewers' organisation SIBA is a key milestone on the road back from multi-national status.

And Magic Rock is seemingly going from strength to strength, exporting to 17 countries, with an expanded

range of products and an annual output of 2.7 million pints, many of which are downed in their impressive on-site taproom. "The whole reason we opened a taproom was to serve the local community," says Andrew. "We're looking to double down on that now; serving the community was always one of our priorities but now it's top of the list.

"Essentially we are finding our feet as independents again. There's a greater level of consistency now, but we do still sometimes ask ourselves, 'What would we have done ten years ago?'"

 Salty Kiss (5%)

It's an unintended consequence of the phenomenal mission of the Campaign for Real Ale that brewers have been given the confidence to experiment in a variety of styles, stretching beyond established boundaries the range of beers now brewed in Britain. Which is how we get a sour German-style Gose, flavoured with gooseberry, sea buckthorn, rosehips and sea salt, created in Huddersfield in collaboration with the Danish brewer Kissmeyer.

Originally from Goslar in Lower Saxony, Gose is a regional speciality first brewed over 1,000 years ago. Made with at least 50% wheat malt, it is similar in style to other wheat beers, Belgian Witbiers and German Weisses, with the obvious difference that it uses salt water in the brew. Light-bodied and slightly carbonated, Salty Kiss pours a pale hazy gold, and though a little saltiness can be discerned in the aroma, its true nature only emerges in the taste. Here your palate is treated to a sour fruity saltiness, with a dazzling array of fruit salad tastes – apple, apricot and banana, and just a suggestion of coriander.

Mallinsons Brewery

Unit 1 Waterhouse Mill, 65-71 Lockwood Road, Huddersfield, HD1 3QU;
T: 01484 654301; W: drinkmallinsons.co.uk; E: info@drinkmallinsons.co.uk;
🄵 @Mallinsons Brewing Company; 🄧 @Mallinsons; 🄾 mallinsonsbrewingco

Huddersfield favourites Mallinsons have been going for a decade and a half now, and stepped up production with a move to a new 15-barrel plant in 2012.

Rather than having permanent beers, Mallinsons produces a rolling core range which usually includes a couple of session-strength cask ales devoted to a particular hop variety and a number of key kegs.

The brewery took Beer of the Festival five times in a row at Huddersfield's Oktoberfest and can usually be found in the best local beer houses – including the Sportsman and the Grove – but they're widely distributed across the north.

It's worth seeking out **Motueka (3.9%)**, whose name honours the hop variety which lends citric aroma to a significant beer of only moderate strength.

Other favourites include the sharply bitter **Mosaic** (4%), orange-accented **Amarillo** (4.2%) and the pale gold tangerine-accented **Summit** (3.9%).

Malton Brewery

5 Navigation Wharf, Malton, North Yorkshire,
YO17 7AA; T: 07946 776613;
W: maltonbrewery.com; E: horsetownbeers@
gmail.com; 🐦 @maltonbrewery

Brewing started on the banks of the Derwent
in Malton in 1767; this new brewery, based
in a grade II listed building, maintains this
long tradition and was named best new
business at the Ryedale Business Awards in
2017.

But it was the introduction of their
Yorkshire Pudding Beer (3.6%) that
brought them most firmly into the public
consciousness, coupled with its success in
Aldi's Next Big Thing contest. The brewery
website claims that "there is half a Yorkshire
Pudding in every bottle" of this new beer,
as though this rather unappealing prospect
were something to boast about. Thankfully,
there is no evidence of the Sunday roast
delicacy in this bright and zesty, supremely
easy-drinking golden ale which now has
national distribution through the budget
supermarket chain.

As we go to press, this runaway success
has seen the suspension of all the other
Malton Brewery products, and the closure of
their online store.

Marlowe Beer Project

1 Mount Pisgah, Otley, LS21 3DX;
🅕 📷 @marlowebeerproject; 🐦 @marlowebeers

A sister brewery to Chevin Brew Co and brewing at the same premises,
Marlowe have been active on social media for some years. But the only
beer I've caught up with is the gently sour, cloudy and wheaty **Zenith
Saison** (6.5%) which I found at a recent beer festival in Otley. It's good;
they should do more...

Meanwood Brewery

8a Stonegate Road, Meanwood, Leeds, LS6 4HY; T: 0113 3185821;
W: themeanwoodbrewery.com; E: sales@themeanwoodbrewery.com;
🅕 🅧 🅞 *@meanwoodbrewery*

"This used to be a brothel," says Justin Keenan, showing us around Meanwood Brewery in north Leeds. The building – originally part of the city's tram terminus – now welcomes punters of a very different kind who seek only the sensual pleasures of great beer brewed on the premises.

Brothers Baz and Graeme Phillips started brewing in their garage before decanting the operation into this splendid two-floor bar and brewhouse in a suburb where a host of new premises have created a fabulous little bar crawl to rival anything the city can offer.

Undeterred by lockdown, the brewery invested in a brand-new kit, increasing capacity from five to ten barrels, and working with distributors to extend their reach well beyond their LS6 heartland. Even so, Terminus, the convivial family-friendly, dog-friendly space next door, remains the perfect place to sample the entire range, as a friend and I did early in 2023.

Volare (4.2%) is a crisp and accessible Italian-style lager; wheat-heavy **Bubo** (4.9%) is an interesting hybrid, somewhere between a witbier and an IPA.

Determined to explore all of beer's many taste experiences, the brothers expand the range almost weekly and recent creations include the imaginative **Wastrel** (4.2%), which uses sloe gin to give an extra edge to the refreshing and surprisingly easy-drinking gose.

ENEMY OF MY ENEMY
HASKAPA SOUR IPA
5.0% ABV

AS WITHIN, SO WITHOUT
EAST COAST PALE
CASCADE/SIMCOE
4.5% ABV

AS ABOVE, SO BELOW
EAST COAST PALE
CASCADE/MOSAIC
4.5% ABV

TRAINING UNDER
THE INFLUENCE
SMALL SUMMER PALE
STYRIAN WOLF
3.2% ABV

Meanwood love a collaboration, and the sturdy, dry, **Meanlove** (5.5%), a golden West Coast IPA packed with the zest of fresh oranges, is the fruit of a hook-up with east Leeds newcomers Piglove. The softly-spoken hazy pale **Stupid Cluepid** (4.5%) was the result of a collaboration with Clue Records.

STUPID CLUEPID
EXTRA PALE
4.5%

Others I've tried in the past include the amber **Shapeshifter** (5.1%) based on the hybrid ale-lager-style California Common; the big juicy New England IPA **Pilgrim** (6.6%); dry and fizzy saison **Trickster** (7.3%), the seductive oak-aged porter **Black Goddess** (4.9%), and **Exile** (3.4%), which twists the Berliner weisse genre with blackberries and oats.

But our evening ends with **Four Lights** (8.8%), a hazy amber double IPA with deep biscuit notes, a pronounced bitterness and a rich warming nature whose insulating influence lasts us all the way home.

WASTREL
SLOE GIN GOSE
4.2%

 Herald (3.9%)

Our evening working through the Meanwood range began with this dry-hopped but malt-forward golden ale, gently bitter, dry and slightly fruity and a perfect overture for an evening's serious drinking. In summer, this will be an absolute go-to refresher for drinkers enjoying the sun-trap decking outside.

HERALD
DH SESSION PALE
3.9%

Mill Valley Brewery

Unit 10, Woodroyd Mills, South Parade, Cleckheaton, BD19 3AF;
T: 07565 229560; E: info@millvalleybrewery.co.uk; W: millvalleybrewery.co.uk;
🐦 *@millvalley2015;* 🄵 *@millvalleybrewerytap*

The varied programme of live entertainment at an on-site bar draws drinkers to Mill Valley, where production is concentrated on a range of moderate-strength ales including the benign and gently amber ale hoppy **Luddite** (3.8%) and the light, spicy **Mill Blonde** (4.2%). Their flagship beer is the tropical fruit session ale **Panther** (4%), while chocolate malt and roast barley lend colour and character to its darker, stronger cousin **Black Panther** (4.6%).

Milltown Brewing Co

The Old Railway Goods Yard, Scar Lane, Milnsbridge, Huddersfield, HD3 4PE;
T: 01422 610579; W: milltownbrewing.co.uk;
E: contact@milltownbrewing.co.uk; 🄵 🐦 *@milltownbrewing*

Before this was a brewery, even before it was a railway goods yard, these premises were stables for delivery horses. The four-barrel plant was established here in 2011 and the beers regularly feature in Huddersfield pubs and those inside a 15-mile radius.

I took the opportunity to try several on a recent visit to the wonderful Traveller's Rest at Meltham, the brewery's second pub, which has wonderful views across the surrounding countryside.

Black Jack (4.5%) is a porter with some nice chocolatey notes; there's a touch of spice to the refreshing **Platinum Blonde** (4%) while **Tiger's Tail** (4.1%) is that refreshing rarity, a genuinely sessionable IPA.

But my favourite was the deep copper-coloured **Weaver's** (3.8%), a traditional Yorkshire bitter, with some crisp, nutty, biscuity notes and a creamy head which holds its firm identity, lacing the side of the glass.

Close by here, the Dusty Miller at Longwood, with its stunning Colne Valley views, remains the brewery tap.

Mithril Ales

Aldbrough St John, Richmond, DL11 7TL; T: 01325 374817;
W: mithrilales.blogspot.com; E: mithril58@btinternet.com

Rather than stick to a core range, brewer Pete Fenwick seems to have a restless spirit for experimentation, his regular blog posts announcing his newest creations and where to find them. Pubs in the very north of the county, and others over the border in County Durham and Northumberland, are the best places to seek out his handiwork. I found rugby-themed **Between The Posts** (3.8%) at the High Force Hotel, after a walk down to the waterfall. Though of only moderate strength, this combined the substantial and long-lasting bitterness of grapefruit with some of the sourness you might expect of a naturally-fermented Belgian beer.

Molson Coors

Tower Brewery, Wetherby Road, Tadcaster, North Yorks, LS24 9JR;
W: molsoncoors.com; E: info@molsoncoors.com

Global giant Molson Coors brews the proverbial shedload of beers, including huge brands like Carling and Fosters. The Tower Brewery, established in 1882 and owned by numerous companies over the past 140 years, is now used to produce beers such as **Caffreys** (4.5%) and **Stones Bitter** (3.7%), as well as giving rival Carlsberg a Yorkshire home for the once-dominant local behemoth **Tetley Bitter** (3.6%).

Morton Collins Brewing

The Star Inn, 42 Standbridge Lane, Wakefield, WF2 7DY; T: 01924 253659;
E: gedmorton@aol.com; **f** *@morton_collins_brewing_company*

After being limited to appearances at local beer festivals, taking over the tenancy at the excellent Star Inn in Sandal gave Ged Morton and Sam Collins a permanent outlet for their microbrewery which began production in 2016.

A visit early in 2023 found a great selection of cask ales on the bar, including three from Morton Collins. They included the session IPA **Rocket** (4.1%) and **Ginger Monkey** (3.5%), so new that its pump clip was hand-written. I went instead for the refreshing pale ale **Expansion** (4%) which announced its presence with a firm bite on the palate, followed by bags of bittersweet orange and just a twist of spice.

I've not seen it in a while, but the remarkable story behind **Maharajah** IPA (5.1%) bears repetition. In 1872, Manchester's Belle Vue Zoo bought an elephant called Maharajah from an Edinburgh menagerie, but he proved a reluctant traveller and destroyed a railway carriage. Eventually, it was decided he would have to walk, and was accompanied on the 200-mile trek by the great-great-grandfather of Ged's wife. This lavishly-hopped fresh, crisp, floral and bitter IPA was unveiled to mark the second anniversary of their takeover at the Star.

Nailmaker Brewing Co

Unit 9, Darton Business Park, Darton, S75 5QX; T: 01226 380893;
W: www.nailmakerbrewing.co
E: beer@nailmakerbrewing.co; **f** **y** **◎** *@nailmakerbrewco*

Paleton (4%), an elegantly-named tribute to the Tour de Yorkshire, was the first to be produced by Nailmaker, which took over where the mothballed Two Roses had left off. The cyclists may be long gone, but this light and citrusy session ale, packed with mandarin, lemon, lime, grapefruit and gooseberry remains a firm favourite.

Its eight-barrel plant, under the same ownership as nearby pubs the Talbot Inn, Anvil Arms and Wentworth Arms, has taken on some of the old Two Roses recipes, while creating some new ones of its own. The name reflects local heritage and industry; the 1841 census shows that there were many more nailmakers locally than miners. The brewery occupies part of an old carpet mill located next to the River Dearne.

Brewed with Cardinal hops, **Cardinal Sin** (4.4%) is a lovely tropical fruit

refresher, while dark chocolate and coffee combine to luxurious effect in **Clout Stout** (5%). Pale ales **Chinook** (4%), **Cascade** (4.2%) and **Mosaic** (4%) each showcase a single hop, while New Zealand's Nelson Sauvin hop lends grape and gooseberry to the lovely pale ale **Auckland** (4%). **Anvil Porter** (4%) revives Two Roses' generously chocolatey Heron Porter.

A beautifully refurbished brewery tap and shop allows drinkers to view the brewery and on-site distillery – as well as purchase bottled and 'bag-in-box' beers to take away.

RECOMMENDED **Chocolate Safari** (5.5%)

They call this a Triple Chocolate Stout; it derives its silky richness from a combination of chocolate malt, organic cacao nibs from the island of Sao Tome, off the African coast, and lashings of extra chocolate. It's a collaboration with Wakefield's own Couer de Xocolat and bathes the palate in a lovely, faintly sweet but slightly whisky-ish blend of ginger, chocolate, and just a hint of smoke.

Neepsend Brew Co

Unit 13, 92 Burton Rd, Neepsend, Sheffield, S3 8DA; T: 0114 3605889;
W: neepsendbrewco.com; E: sales@neepsendbrewco.com;
@neepsendbrewco

The start of the pandemic saw Neepsend move to new premises in Burton Road, a former industrial location now home to some of the coolest local businesses.

And in August 2022, head brewer Gavin Martin left for pastures new, with assistant brewer Harry Geeves stepping into the breach. If the name's familiar, that's because for ten years he was the creative force behind Barnsley's Geeves Brewery. "We've been fortunate to see a steady growth in production since the pandemic," he tells me. "We began canning our beers in-house at the start of lockdown. These have been very well received and can be found at most bottle shops, along with some pubs and restaurants around the city."

Crisp and fruity **Alcis** (4.2%) is a session IPA while New England pale **Myron** (4.2%) picked up the bronze medal for Champion Beer at the Sheffield Beer Festival in 2022.

Blonde (4%)

This mellow and sessionable pale ale is the flagship Neepsend beer. Hopped with Brewer's Gold, Chinook and Cascade, this delicate blonde is mellow and easy-drinking, low in bitterness and with a crisp dry finish. All the Neepsend pump clips feature Ball Street Bridge, a local landmark which is in sight of the brewery. It's actually the second – the original 1856 bridge was washed away in the disastrous Sheffield flood eight years later.

Nightjar Brew Co

2 Richmond House, Caldene Business Park, Mytholmroyd, HX7 5QL;
T: 07412 008221; W: nightjarbrew.co.uk; E: matt@nightjarbrew.co.uk;
🅵 🅳 *@nightjarbrewco;* 🅾 *@nightjar_brew_co*

When I first visited these premises, they were home to the Slightly Foxed
Brewery, but a change of name, direction and beers some years ago has
transformed the brewery's fortunes, spreading a love for a fresh roster of
ales across Calderdale and beyond. Their mix of cask and keg ales can
now be found along the M62 corridor, to the Lakes and Derbyshire, while
wholesalers ensure their beers get much further afield. "There's a little
pocket of bars in Hove that always take our kegs," says owner Matt Bell.
"Things are going well."

His positivity is tempered by a sense of survivors' guilt: "It's really
concerning that we've lost so many breweries during the pandemic –
and so many of them were our friends. A lot have succumbed. It almost
makes you feel slightly guilty for getting through it."

Nightjar owner Matt Bell (right) and brewer Jake Bartleet-Perry

Nightjar's best-known beer is the NEIPA **Lost in Ikea** (4.2%). "A licensee complained that it wasn't coming through the lines properly just the morning after he'd put it on. He later rang back really embarrassed. It was empty; it had sold out in two hours the night before."

There's clearly a real attention to design here, from the beautifully stylised nightjar's wing of the logo, to the wonderful images of the cans. Of these, one which caught my eye was the biscotti vanilla cake stout **Half Can Half Biscuit** (6.8%), the name an homage to Britain's greatest post-punk ironic comedy folk band. It's a small field, I guess, but the beer is wonderful – a luxurious blend of dark chocolate, rich chewy malt and the indulgent sweetness of dark cherries. The big-bodied hazy pale **Astral Matrix** (8%) is a potent, pungent soup of cloves and grapefruit, bitter pear drops, blue cheese and bags of yeast.

Other choices include the smooth and chocolatey oatmeal stout **Cosmonaut** (4.4%) and its stronger, sweeter, porridge-thick, dark chocolate cousin **Supernova** (6.9%). "We do a good range of regulars, occasionals and 'hit and run' beers," says Matt. They enjoy a collaboration too. The first of these, launched in March 2019, was with wheat beer specialist Eyes Brewing – sadly no longer with us – and was called **Plum Dunk Da Funk** (6.5%), an imaginative plum dunkelweizen brewed with mountains of real plums, molasses and star anise. There are plenty more, besides.

The two brewery taps – Bradford's Exchange Craft Beer House and the Nightjar tap in Hebden Bridge, are reliable places to sample the many and varied delights of this re-invented brewery. Hove too, if you're down that way.

Return of the Sky Gods (9.8%)

Brutally strong, yet delicately easy to drink, this wonderful imperial stout was one of the absolute nuggets I unearthed during a week-long research trip to complete this book. The aroma is rich coffee, and some of this is maintained in an espresso martini taste, given added richness by roasted cocoa nibs and creamy lactose, to which luxurious sweetness and body are added by a shedload of Madagascan vanilla pods. Beers as dangerous as this should probably be illegal.

Nook Brewhouse

Victoria Square, Holmfirth, HD9 2DN; T: 01484 682373;
W: thenookbrewhouse.co.uk; E: office@thenookbrewhouse.co.uk;
🅕 @thenookbrewhouse; 🐦 @Nookbrewhouse

In 2009 a local brewing tradition was revived in the heart of picturesque Holmfirth with the opening of a brewhouse behind The Rose and Crown pub, where an ancient brewery once stood. A cool cellar built deep below the waterline of the neighbouring River Ribble is perfect for conditioning the beer.

Documents and deeds on display in the pub highlight the history of the site and a proud brewing heritage which dates back to 1754. For many of those years, the pub has been known simply as The Nook.

Their cask-conditioned ales can be found in pubs and bars and at beer festivals across the north. It's easy to spot their bottled beers and pump clips adorned with the grotesque cartoons of the Nook pump clips – each apparently based on some of the pub's regulars.

Regular brews include sessionable, mid-brown – and not especially bitter – **Yorks Bitter** (3.7%), and the malty, caramelly **Red** (4.5%).

There's a flowery aroma to the pale golden **Blond** (4.5%), with some nice fruity notes on the palate, lemon and apricot; the sharp and tangy **Baby Blond** (3.8%) is its more sessionable offspring. There's a golden and floral **Best** (4.2%) and the full-bodied, slightly treacly **Oat Stout** (5.2%). The list is completed with a good selection of occasional ales and specials.

🍺 **Nook'y Brown** (4.9%)

You might think this is the brewery's own pastiche of the north-eastern favourite – albeit a beer which was long brewed in Tadcaster, and now in Holland. But at 4.9% ABV the Nook version is a shade stronger than the Geordie beer and perhaps actually a shade or two darker. It has real body and substance, and a mellow, dried fruit, toffee-ish taste with some initial zestiness and a lovely warming, bitter finish.

North Brewing

Springwell, Buslingthorpe Lane, Leeds, LS7 2DF; T: 0113 345 3290; W: northbrewing.com; E: sales@northbrewing.com; 🄵 *@northbrewingleeds;* 𝕏 📷 *@northbrewco*

North Bar Group was a driving force behind the craft beer movement in Leeds. From its modest beginnings as a small bar in Briggate, the group catalysed a significant change in the city's drinking culture, introducing a public weaned on Tetley's and Sam Smith's to some of the amazing, interesting and occasionally baffling beers available from around the world.

From Briggate, the group built organically, each expansion into new premises keeping roughly in pace with a burgeoning reputation for quality beer, knowledgeable staff and laid-back atmosphere. It was perhaps only a matter of time before North was further seized by the spirit of the times to open its own brewery. Initially based at Taverner's Walk in Sheepscar, during the pandemic they moved to impressive new premises – a converted 21,000-square-foot former Victorian tannery a half mile away in Buslingthorpe Lane. Here the increased capacity and a big lively taproom meets an ever-growing demand.

Their entry-level beer, the laid-back and sessionable **Vanishing Point** (3.8%) is a bright and crisp blonde with some modest fruit flavours, and began life as their very first beer, Prototype, initially brewed with Roosters. It remains my staple choice during regular Friday night visits to the rather lovely Further North in Chapel Allerton.

Though there are some fruity aromatic notes to the pale amber, soft

and juicy IPA **Transmission** (6.9%), it's only when it hits the palate that it really starts throwing its weight around. Its strength manifests itself in an immediate blast of big-tasting hops and its full-on bitterness develops into a complex cocktail of grapefruit and passion fruit, almost as though the brew has been spiked with a syrupy concentrate. Curiously for an IPA – whose roots lie in the need for a cooling, refreshing, revitalising beer for the troops – its formidable potency lends some surprising warming qualities.

Fresh tropical pale **Pinata** (4.5%) is a massive seller. Characteristically for North, it packs plenty of fruit flavour – mango, tangerine, grapefruit – into a beer of only modest strength. The mouthfeel is oily, creamy, rich, and the significant sweet citric qualities are tempered by some bitter hops.

Joining forces with the club fanzine to celebrate Leeds United's promotion to the Premier League in 2020 resulted in the rather similar **Square Ball** (4.5%) which doubtless won over new fans to the North Brewing cause.

Their **Triple Fruited Gose** (4.5%) was crowned Champion Keg Beer at SIBA's 2023 Awards. The brewery produces several different iterations of this salty, wheaty, northern European style, each buzzing with a distinct flavour profile. The one my expert tasters tried was the white and pink guava and mango version, where the pleasant, slightly tart fruit notes balanced the sourness in a rich, musky, earthy brew. Said one: "Waves of guava-infused sweetness sashay with mango, oats and salt in a celebration of flavours that my head warned me would never work, yet on a balmy spring evening my mouth disagreed."

Some occasionals and specials allow the brewers to stretch themselves into something new. Dense, peachy, vinous saison **A Hymn for the Fields** (8%) and barrel-aged Imperial Stout **Moersleutel** (11%) typify their experimental Field Recordings series, while a basket of malts combine with cinnamon, nutmeg, cacao and vanilla in the smooth, roasty and massively festive-flavoured Christmas beer **Endless Ends** (10%).

Their long list of collaborators goes from traditional family brewers like Oldham's JW Lees to Bristol craftsters Left Handed Giant, Leeds's own Northern Bloc ice cream to Swedish hipsters Dugges.

It may no longer be brewed, but the potent **Triple IPA** (10%), the result of a collaboration with Uiltje Brewery in Haarlem, is emblematic of North's commitment to innovation and quality. When I tried this at Further North, the barman decanted it into the broad bowl of a large brandy glass, whose shape held in so ferocious an aroma of citrus and hop resins that I almost intoxicated myself by breathing its fumes. The smallest sip lathers the tongue with a thick soup of lime, lemon and grapefruit concentrated to vindaloo strength, warming the throat and lulling you towards an etherised unconsciousness. It's as though the Anglo-Dutch brew team would like to congratulate you on choosing their beer by giving you a big high five. In the face. With a chair.

🍺 Full Fathom 5 (6.5%)

It was at North Brewing's first brewery taproom that I made acquaintance with this coffee and coconut porter – and now often turn to it as a last beer of the night at Further North. Unlike some brews which go down these routes, here neither of those rich flavours is allowed to dominate. Instead, the brewer has created a luscious, jet-black, velvety ale which is still essentially a porter, but with enough depth to allow the coffee and the coconut to lend their influence. At the same time, they contribute to a silky, creamy texture, which perhaps at first serves to disguise its premium strength, though its significant power is finally revealed as it passes down the throat into a long dry aftertaste.

North Riding Brewery

Unit 6, Barkers Lane, Snainton, YO13 9BD; T: 01723 864845;
W: northridingbrewery.com; E: stuart@northridingbrewery.com;
🅕 @northridingbreweryltd; 🅣 @northridingbrew

It's now five years since NRB decamped from East Ayton to Snainton a few miles further west of Scarborough, where bigger premises offered the opportunity to expand. American hops are key to Stuart Neilson's recipes with his fruity pale ales **Citra** (4.5%) and **Mosaic** (4.3%) named after big-selling varieties.

Scarborough's excellent North Riding Brewpub, run by Stuart's wife Karen, offers a home to these beers and plenty more. It was here that I made acquaintance with the grassy, pleasantly floral and straw-coloured pale ale **Cascade** (4%), though time and drink-drive considerations prevented me trying the more powerful **IPA** (6.2%) and **Cheesecake Stout** (5.5%).

North Riding Brewpub

161-163 North Marine Rd, Scarborough, YO12 7HU; T: 01723 370004;
🅕 @northridingbrewpub; 🅣 @north_riding

While North Riding licensee Karen Neilson's husband operates North Riding Brewery, her son John operates the small brewkit in the basement of this multi-CAMRA-award-winning pub. On my visit we tried the big-tasting and full-bodied pale ale **Styrian Wolf** (4.3%). While John chiefly supplies ale for the pub's customers, his casks do occasionally escape to further afield. I made aquaintance with the lovely, rich and treacly black IPA **Artorias** (7%) in Foley's in Leeds; the patriotic pump clip of a St George's shield makes them easy to spot on any bar.

North Yorkshire Brewing

South Gare Court, Redcar, TS10 5BN; T: 01642 497298; W: nybrewery.co.uk;
E: sales@nybrewery.co.uk; **☐** *@NorthYorkshireBreweryLtd*

This brewery has moved around a few times, from Middlesbrough to Pinchinthorpe Manor in Guisborough and then in 2017 to this industrial estate close to the North Sea coast.

The name and fearsome fighting skull image of the pump clip of premium bitter **Valhalla** (5.5%) is suggestive of something rather dangerous, though this sweetish malty, caramelly ale is actually rather beautifully soporific.

Deep brown bitter **Flying Herbert** (4.7%), with its tangy bitter marmalade notes, remains the flagship product, while pale lager-ale cross **White Lady** (4.7%) recalls a spectre reputed to walk the corridors of Pinchinthorpe, perhaps wondering where the brewery has gone.

The move to new premises south of Leeds has allowed Northern Monk to expand production to meet rising demand

Northern Monk

Unit 7, Sydenham Road, Leeds, LS11 9RU; T: 0113 243 6430; W: northernmonk.com; E: bookings@northernmonk.com;
🅕 *@northernmonkbrewco;* 🅧 *@NMBCo;* 🅘 *@northernmonk*

Northern Monk is one of the stellar success stories of British brewing. Just ten years after being founded in a cellar in 2013, Northern Monk is now exporting worldwide. The brewery moved into the old flax store of Marshall's Mill in 2014, its utilitarian red-brick bulk lending itself beautifully to brewkit, bar and events space. Its upstairs Refectory has become a regular stopping point on my regular beer and heritage walks around the city centre; the Egyptian-influenced colonnaded frontage of nearby Temple Mills invokes gasps of surprise.

The brewery's success is based on quality, a nod to traditional monastic brewing values – and an ethos of providing crafted, well-thought-out ales, with a progressive approach to ingredients and techniques. Heading to the bar you are almost overwhelmed by choice. The back bar has more lines than a sonnet and almost all are Northern Monk.

The core range includes a host of pales – the tangerine-dominated session IPA **Eternal** (4.1%), the gentle and pineapple-accented **Faith** (5.4%) and hazy tropical fruit **Heathen** (7.2%) – to which were added in 2019 the fresh low-alcohol **Striding Edge** (2.8%) and gluten-free IPA

Origin (5.7%). Jet-black **Northern Star** (5.9%) is a strong mocha porter – suggestions of dark chocolate and hazelnut and ground coffee beans lend a luxurious decadence which might surprise the London wharf and market porters who once made this style their very own.

A series of Patrons Projects beers fosters collaboration, creativity and community between artists, athletes and creatives across the north. The juicy sessionable IPA **Starburst** (5.2%) arose from a partnership with Scottish print studio Risotto; a cocktail of Australian hops powers the tropical spicy **Love** (4.8%), developed with Leeds tattoo artist Demondance.

The expansion into the former Leeds Brewery premises south west of the city centre allows Northern Monk to brew up to 18 beers at a time, while the second Refectory in Manchester's Northern Quarter expands this evolving story yet further.

I have no doubt that such industry would be admired by those who who founded Holbeck as one of the workshops of the world. Should John Marshall's ghost ease himself from the ancient brickwork to walk the bare wooden boards of his old flax store, I think he might just approve.

Brewer Cat Mowat in creative mode at Northern Monk

New World (6.2%)

Northern Monk's brewing talents stretch from the most low-alcohol refreshers to the high-octane piledrivers; at 6.2% this big-tasting India Pale Ale comes from somewhere mid-range. This cloudy pale ale lures the unwary with a pleasant, fruity, flowery aroma – all pineapple and peach – before really throwing its weight around on the palate. It announces itself on the tongue with some earthy, almost dank bitterness and there's enough rich oiliness to the texture to suggest this might be even stronger than its ABV. There are still some juicy, citric notes, but these are fleshed out by the firmer characteristics of pine resins, fresh herbs and even a suggestion of tobacco. As a well-constructed ale it is a perfect example of everything that Northern Monk stands for. But it's not for the faint-hearted.

Old Mill Brewery

Mill Street, Snaith, DN14 9HU; T: 01405 861813; W: oldmillbrewery.co.uk;
E: sales@oldmillbrewery.co.uk; **f** *OldMillBrewerySnaith;* **𝕏 ◎** *@oldmillbrewery*

Around 150 years ago, Snaith was well served by brewers and maltsters, though the emergence of the major breweries in nearby Tadcaster saw the trade die out. Only with the opening of Old Mill Brewery in 1983 did this great craft return to a town whose origins lie before the Norman Conquest.

Almost four decades on, the brewery was in need of a shake-up, as new brewery manager Ian Cowling explained: "Everything was wrong." From the milling machine whose inefficiencies saw 30% of the malt having to be thrown away, to the fact they had been buying poor-quality cleaning chemicals, work was urgently needed. "It was a bit of a mess. I'd been brought in to increase production, but to do that we needed to spend money."

A £100,000 investment from the Wetherell family, who have owned the brewery since its inception, has allowed Ian to make some much-needed changes – a new grist case, chilling units, heat exchanger, water treatment plant, barrel washing kit and more – as Old Mill heads towards its 40th birthday.

One thing that won't change is its flagship traditional **Bitter** (3.9%), which has now been joined in the core range by premium pale ale **Styrian Wolf** (4.2%). The malty, coffee and chocolate porter **La Bolsa** (4.5%) is an occasional special. All are under the stewardship of Michael Winnyczuk, who has been head brewer here for the past year. "He's one of the best microbrewers in the business," says Ian. "The quality has really gone up."

That quality is reflected in the easy-going pale citric **Jester** (3.8%), one of the newest additions to the range, which draws on the rich tropical fruit and blackcurrant characteristics of UK-grown Jester hops.

The recent acquisition of the Bay Horse at Burythorpe brings Old Mill's tied estate up to 18 pubs; reciprocal trading arrangements with Heineken and drinks wholesalers HB Clark take their beers the length and breadth of the UK.

But work still needs to be done. "Right now I'm taking out a pump that has been there for 32 years," says Ian. "We're just hoping it can be repaired or all the pipework under the brewkit will have to change. Everything is a challenge – but I'm really enjoying it."

On The Edge

Woodseats, Sheffield; T: 07854 983197; W: ontheedgebrew.com;
E: ontheedgebrew@gmail.com; 🐦 *@ontheedgebrew*

Thomas Richards and Luisa Golob operate a tiny half-barrel brewing plant in their kitchen. No brew is the same as the last and the beers go to pubs such as the The Broadfield in Abbeydale Road and the interesting Mallard on Worksop station. A string of awards from local festivals underlines the quality from this most micro of microbreweries.

BUTTERLEY
YORKSHIRE BITTER 3.8%

EXCELSIUS
DRY-HOPPED PALE ALE 5.2%

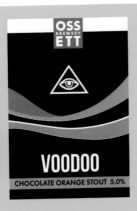

VOODOO
CHOCOLATE ORANGE STOUT 5.0%

Ossett Brewery

Low Mill Road, Ossett, WF5 8ND; T: 01924 261333;
W: www.ossett-brewery.co.uk; E: brewery@ossett-brewery.co.uk;
🔵 🐦 📷 *@ossettbrewery*

Almost 25 years of steady growth has seen Ossett built from a microbrewery into one of the region's major players with a string of more than 30 pubs, nationwide distribution, an ambitious craft beer arm Salt Brewing, and three local microbreweries – Rat, Fernandes and Riverhead – added to the fold.

The success is founded on a trio of solidly performing real ales: amiable, malty **Yorkshire Blonde** (3.9%), multi-award-winning crisp, dry American Pale Ale **Silver King** (4.3%) and premium pale ale **Excelsius** (5.2%). Seasonal and limited edition ales extend the choice still further.

Sessionable hoppy pale ale **White Rat** (4%) – originally brewed by the Rat Brewery – was re-branded as an Ossett beer four years ago, and sales have soared. Following that lead, Fernandes' chocolate orange stout **Voodoo** (5%) and Riverhead's gentle bitter **Butterley** (3.8%) have moved

WHITE RAT
HOPPY PALE ALE 4.0%

SILVER KING
AMERICAN PALE ALE 4.3%

YORKSHIRE
BLONDE
PALE SESSION ALE 3.9%

from their respective homes to become part of the mothership brand.

"These shining stars of our microbreweries enjoy an ever-growing fan base, but increasing production in their home breweries was not possible," says Ossett boss Jamie Lawson. "Demand for White Rat is now pretty much on par with our leading brew, Yorkshire Blonde, which is quite incredible. As true White Rat fans know, we have long brewed it successfully at Ossett and I can also reassure Black Voodoo and Butterley fans that the character of the brews remains untouched. We have simply tweaked the design but certainly not the beer."

Ossett's excellent chain of Hop pubs – and bars such as Archie's and Craft Asylum in Leeds are the ideal places to immerse yourself in the whole Ossett experience, while the rapid expansion of the Salt brand, which now includes two venues in London, is spreading the word about a confident, ambitious, passionate brewery which is doing all the important things right.

A visit to the Hop in Leeds, set into the brooding underground red-brick cathedral of the dark arches, where water rushes beneath and trains rumble overhead, is a chance to marvel at the ingenuity of Victorian engineering.

Outhouse Brewing

Unit 16a, Redbrook Business Park, Wilthorpe Road, Barnsley, S75 1JN; T: 07572 164446; W: outhousebrewing.co.uk; E: info@outhousebrewing.co.uk; 🅵 🆈 @outhousebrewing

Andy Jones's beers take advantage of spare capacity on the Jolly Boys Brewery kit, but since trying the steady-away pale **Garden Shed** (4%) a couple of years ago, it's become hard to know if this cuckoo's still flying.

Pennine Brewing Co

Well Hall Farm, Bedale, DL8 2PX; T: 01677 470111;
W: pennine-brewing.co.uk; E: sales@pennine-brewing.co.uk;
🄵 *@penninebrewingco;* 🄳 *@PennineBrewing;* 🄾 *@penninebrewco*

Pennine decamped in 2013 from Batley in 2013 to the edge of the rolling Vale of Mowbray, a bucolic stretch of low-lying land between the North York Moors and the Hambleton Hills to the east and the Yorkshire Dales to the west. A dizzying and dazzling domain of special and seasonal ales means they have always got something different to offer to augment long-standing favourites such as the sparkling **Amber Necker** (3.9%) and the creamy dried-fruit golden ale **Scapegoat** (4.2%).

As I did before the pandemic, in 2022 I had the enjoyable task of judging the best locally-produced beer for the Taste of Herriot Country Awards. It was a tough task, as there were some really strong contenders. The winner was Bayonet's lovely One Pip Wonder, but I gave an honourable mention to Pennine Brewing and particularly their rich, dark and treacly **Hog Man's Stout** (4.4%).

Attractive ruby session ale **Northland** (4.1%) is a well-balanced ale of dark fruit and toffee aromas, whose significant sharp, hoppy character emerges in the last knockings, but Pennine's standout performer is the blonde and caramelly **Hair of the Dog** (3.9%) which has garnered a string of awards and is a 'must-have' beer wherever you find it.

🍺 Millie George (4.1%)

Styled as a 'blonde with attitude', this is named after the daughter of the brewers; bright and highly-carbonated, it looks for all the world like Lucozade, glimmering attractively in the glass. It is very much aimed at the sessionable end of the market, tripping across the palate with a delicate, thirst-quenching, easy-going nature. That buzzy, almost fizzy appearance yields some bready notes in the aroma; on the palate it has a friendly, only faintly hoppy nature, with just a little bitterness in the finish. In this companionable character it never quite manages to throw off the impression of being just like Lucozade, a perfect reviving tonic for the thirsty.

Piglove Brewing Co  New

Unit 6, Cross Green Lane, Leeds, LS9 8LJ; T: 07718 630467;
W: piglovebrewing.com; 🅕 *@piglove_brewing_co;*
🐦 *@piglove_brewing;* 📷 *@piglovebrewing*

A love so big – perhaps too big, too raw, too passionate – is not a phenomenon for which we buttoned-up Brits have ever needed an expression. Those less repressed Venezuelans call this 'cochino amor', or 'piglove', and this new brewery just east of Leeds city centre is starting to see the word take root.

Established in 2019, Piglove is the social centre for the Leeds Climate Innovation District, an energy-efficient development of homes, offices and green infrastructure in Cross Green. Its riverside bar has proved a huge draw: "Most of our brewery production goes to the bar during the summer," says Head Brewer Richard Jones. When we spoke late in 2022, he was looking forward to the arrival of new tanks to double production capacity.

Richard came to Piglove by way of Bath Brewery and the University of Leeds Real Ale Society. "They took a chance on me," he admits.

A Latin American influence hangs heavy over a range of beers divided into three groups. The Maloca series, named after a traditional Amazonian home, also references the dwelling as a symbol for mother earth and for knowledge. The aromatic session IPA **Omnia** (4.5%) draws woody sweetness from Palo Santo, a 'Holy Wood' reputed for its spiritually purifying properties. This typifies the Piglove ethos: "We use South American flavours all the time," says Richard. "It's our fifth ingredient in every brew."

The Qaawa series is inspired by the holistic Mayan approach to mind and body. Wheaty, pineapply ale **Hypermnesia** (4.9%) – named for the intuition that something bad is about to happen – draws earthy, peppery character from the Amazon spice Achiote. Acerola berries lend an influence to the piney, only moderately bitter but seriously potent New England IPA **Spirits Arise** (7.4%).

Beers in the Phantasticum series each have the woody aftertaste of the rainforest plant Chuchuhuasi, renowned for its healing and mystical properties. **Universe** (5.6%) is a fruity sour, **Hop Healer** (6.5%) a grainy, orangey IPA, **Limbus** (9%) a no-holds-barred, big-bodied aromatic stout.

Beyond Cross Green, city-centre craft ale champions like Wapentake and Friends of Ham have shown this innovative brewery some love, while sending beer off-site for canning is allowing them to infiltrate the off-trade too.

Even so, the mysterious disappearance of co-founder Jesus Moreno in August 2022 cast a long shadow over the brewery. It was only in April 2023 that his body was finally discovered, close to where he had been last seen in Harewood. Piglove's sustained success would be a most fitting memorial to his life and work.

Play Brew

8, Cannon Park Way, Middlesbrough, TS1 5JU; T: 01642 224769;
W: playbrewco.com; E: sales@playbrewco.com; 🇫 🇹 *@playbrewco*

This brewery and taproom opened in 2019; their cans and kegs are already gaining a wide distribution. The only one I've tried so far is the potent, fragrant pastry stout **Choco Profiterole** (6.7%), a rich and creamy, indulgent sweet blend of chocolate and vanilla. If this is typical of their output, they'll go far.

Pumphouse Brewing *New*

Unit 10 D, Twydale Business Park Skerne Rd, Driffield, YO25 6JX;
T: 07867 584488; E: zsolt@pumphousebrewing.co.uk;
🇫 *@PumphouseBrewingCo*

My last visit to this back-of-beyond location on the outskirts of Driffield was to seek out Butcher's Dog Brewery. Though its town-centre taproom is still running, that brewery has now closed, and my focus has switched a few doors down to Pumphouse, which opened in the summer of 2019 – and quickly became a fabulous local phenomenon.

Theirs is an interesting business model, focused on producing an eclectic selection of small-batch, hand-crafted beer styles from around the world, sold exclusively to locals visiting their own industrial chic taproom.

Having established the beers, they began to invite different street food vendors – and once the taproom started to fill up on Friday and Saturday nights, performances by local musicians built the atmosphere still further. The place quickly became a popular weekend destination; word of mouth ensured that business grew week-on-week.

That was until Covid arrived, but Pumphouse survived by selling take-out to their new but already loyal fanbase. And after surviving the hiatus, the brewery is thriving by offering something genuinely different – with ten ever-changing craft keg beers and a host of different cuisines. At any one

time, there's a stock of at least 20 different beers in the cellar ready to put on as soon as a line runs out at the bar.

"Our focus remains on small-batch brewing," says director Zsolt Hangrad. "This enables the brewer to produce a different, new beer or a variation of an existing brew each time. Experimentation and a constantly evolving selection keeps the patrons engaged and happy."

So while there's no core range here, there are some favourites brewed on a regular basis, but to a slightly different recipe. Even Pumphouse's signature beer, the **Lemongrass IPA** is created with such a varying mixture of citrus and herbs, and to a different malt and yeast bill that its strength can vary from the sessionable 4.5% to the more challenging 6.6%. The **Session Pale** (4.5%-4.9%) is another bestseller, again brewed with a different variety of hop to keep the customers guessing.

Pumphouse have embraced a host of different styles from German **Kolsches** (5-6%) to **Baltic Porters** (7.5-10%), a Caribbean-style **Tropical Stout** (6.5%) to a **Scots Wee Heavy** (6%). "We found that the local water is really suitable for French and Belgian style Saisons and Grisettes," says Zsolt. These range from a **Summer Blonde** (4.5%) to a **Strong Blonde** (7.3%) and **The Devil** (9.8%).

And there's a commitment to authenticity: "Whatever beer we decide to try out, a lot of effort goes into researching the history of the product making sure that the correct yeast, malts, hops and processes are being used to produce a sample true to that style of beer."

Some are aged up to three years for added strength and richness, bringing an extra dimension to the sensory pleasures that Pumphouse is bringing to the lucky folk of YO25.

Quirky Ales

Ash Lane, Garforth, Leeds, LS25 2HG; T: 0113 286 2072; W: quirkyales.com;
E: info@quirkyales.com; 🟦 🟦 *@quirkyales;* 🟦 *@quirkycraftales*

On an industrial estate on the edge of Garforth, hidden away behind low-rise workshops and warehouses, this remarkable little brewery and bar have firmly established themselves in the local community, drawing a regular following to this most unpromising of locations.

It was the brainchild of Mike Quirk who began home brewing in 2015 after handing in his warrant card and looking for something less stressful to do with his time. It soon evolved from the quaint and quirky to the quite extraordinary as Mike upgraded his tiny brewkit to some serious stainless steel and installed it at this unprepossessing warehouse, just outside the centre of Garforth.

It took quite a leap of faith to believe that drinkers would come here to drink, but The Quirky Tap, with its friendly atmosphere and log-burning stove, has become an integral part of the local drinking scene, popular with ramblers and dog walkers. The on-site taproom has just a handful of tables, while other customers stand or head to the outside drinking area.

Mike was joined by Richard Scott in 2017 as the business found its feet; Mike left two years later, leaving it in the safe hands of Richard, co-director Simon Mustill and brewer Aaron Getliffe.

Aaron concentrates on 'Beers of Comfort', though some more off-the-

wall ales are produced in small volumes, testing the palates of an adventurous clientele. Regular guest brew days give all-comers the chance to try their hand at the creative process.

Aaron brews twice a week, and the choice on draught varies from day to day. They often include New Zealand pale **Two Islands** (3.8%) and the more contemporary **IPA Hip Hop** (5.5%), both of which have recently won regional beer festival awards.

Brewer Aaron Getliffe, left, with director Richard Scott

Once poured, **Garforth Porter** (3.5%) is a formidable sight, jet-black with a foaming beige head and some enticing liquorice aromas. But on the palate it's a much more benign proposition, surprisingly soft and blessedly meek with a hint of malt. It trips lightly across the tongue, almost insubstantial and very refreshing and drinkable. Some true quirky character emerges in the finish as you're hit with a late blast of blackberries and dusty old books.

But the pick of the bunch for me is the impressively substantial, rich red-brown **Classic** (5.7%), packed with the sweetness of dark fruit and bonfire toffee and undoubtedly a homage to Theakston's Old Peculier.

The brewery has recently been listed as one of the top ten breweries to visit in Yorkshire and rates a mention in the Lonely Planet Guide. It's open from Thursday to Sunday, and they even manage to shoehorn live acts onto an impromptu stage beside the door, though accommodating anyone bigger than a duo wouldn't leave room for their equipment. Or an audience.

Radiant Brewing

50 Eaton Hill, Leeds, LS16 6SE; W: www.radiantbrewing.co.uk; E: Hello@radiantbrewing.co.uk; 🅕 🅞 @radiantbrewing

Radiant launched late in 2021, and though I enjoyed their zesty **Lemon Cheesecake** ale (4.9%) the following summer – I've heard little since from a brewery whose web address doesn't work, and social media is dormant.

Rat Brewery

40, Chapel Hill, Huddersfield, HD1 3EB;
T: 01484 542400;
W: www.ossett-brewery.co.uk;
E: ratcrafted@rat-brewery.co.uk;
@ratbrewery

The Rat and Ratchet was established as a brewpub in 1994, and though brewing ceased for several years it began again in 2011, following the pub's purchase by regional giants Ossett Brewery. Brewer Paul Spencer, who describes himself as Head Rodent, clearly has a penchant for puns, with beers such as the uber-hopped IPA **Rat Against the Machine** (7%), **Imperial Stout Ratsputin** (7.4%) and bottled barley wine **Grapes Of Rat** (10%).

Regulars include the dark coffee-ish porter **Rat in Black** (4.5%) and the straw-coloured, wine-nosed, New Zealand-hopped **King Rat** (5%) – with beers available in cask and keg.

Most of their beers are distinctive, extreme, and intensely hopped and anything but average, as Paul and fellow brewer Robin Moss experiment with a changing range of beer styles, strengths and ingredients.

Their most famous product has now been squirrelled away to Ossett. Brewed at far greater volume by the parent company, and marketed nationwide, the pale and aromatic flagship bitter **White Rat** (4%) is now infecting all four corners of the UK faster than the Black Death, turning a local infestation into a national plague.

Raven Hill Brewery

Raven Hill Farm, Driffield, YO25 4EG; T: 07979 674573;
W: ravenhillbrewery.com; E: hello@ravenhillbrewery.com;
🆒 🅾 🅾 *@ravenhillbrew; T: @ravenhillbrew*

Relative newcomers when the last edition of the *Yorkshire Beer Bible* was published, Ravenhill is now more firmly established – with cask and keg ales going to the local on-trade, with cans and bottles sold via the on-trade and an on-line store.

There has been something of a shake-up since last time – none of the beers I listed remain on sale, while the designs have taken on a stylised countryside theme, which ties in with the outdoor adventures theme of the website. Saaz hops lend central European influence authenticity to **Alpine** (4.6%), a classic Czech-style lager with some herbal, piney notes.

Mosaic and Cascade bring their much-loved tropical fruit blast to the hazy New England IPA **Explorer** (5.5%) while the mango, tangerine and perhaps even banana of the more potent **Ravine** (6.7%) expand on this theme.

Redscar Brewery

Cleveland Hotel, 9-11 High Street West, Redcar, North Yorks, TS10 1SQ;
T: 01642 513727; W: redscar-brewery.co.uk; 🆒 🅾 *@RedScarBrewery*

My careful calculations have established that Redscar is Yorkshire's most northerly brewery, though it's a matter of metres between its latitude and that of North Yorkshire Brewing across town at Warrenby.

This five-barrel plant concentrates on supplying session beers locally – not least to the popular family-run pub upstairs. Most have single-syllable names, like the slightly thin-tasting entry level **Sands** (3.8%), the more impressive mellow and fruity **Rocks** (4%) and the amber, toffee-ish premium bitter **Beach** (5%).

Richmond Brewing Company

The Old Station, Richmond, DL10 4LD; T: 01748 828266;
W: richmondbrewing.co.uk; E: enquiries@richmondbrewing.co.uk;
🄵 *@richmondbrewingcompany;* 🄳 *@richmondbrewing*

In 2016, new fermenting and conditioning tanks and a bar for visitors to sample the beers doubled the size of the brewery based in Richmond's stunning riverside Victorian railway station which closed to trains in 1969 and is now home to cinemas, galleries and a number of artisan food producers.

Deep brown mild **Swale** (3.7%) divides opinion, according to boss Chris Wallace who adds: "But CAMRA go mad for it." It has some surprising vinegar sharpness on the nose which might easily fool you into thinking this might be a sour Belgian fruit beer. Yet on the palate that soon disappears behind a blanket of malt and toffee, that develops some genuine bitterness as it fades away. Beers of this very moderate strength rarely deliver quite so much. Other beers include the light and golden **Station Ale** (4%), and the dark malty **Drummer Boy** (3.8%).

🍺 **Stump Cross** (4.7%)
The bones of reindeer, bison and wolverines were found in the four miles of Stump Cross Cavern between Pateley Bridge and Grassington, which was discovered by lead miners in the 19th century and is believed to date back almost half a million years. Natural cave water, filtered through the limestone, is added to this premium bitter which pours a rich deep red, with a tight foaming head and some notable suggestions of toffee in the aroma. On the palate, Stump Cross develops some sweetish fruitcakey tastes of cherry and marzipan, with a significant malt presence that trumps any bitter influence from the hops.

Ridgeside Brewery

Unit 24, Penraevon 2 Industrial Estate, Jackson Road, Leeds, LS7 2AW;
T: 07595 380568; W: ridgesidebrewery.co.uk;
E: accounts@ridgesidebrewery.co.uk;
🅕 🅧 *@ridgesidebrewer;* 🅞 *@ridgesidebrewery*

The sad death of Simon Bolderson in 2014 robbed Leeds brewing of a legend. Over just four years, this big-hearted, leonine-maned bear of a man had established Ridgeside's reputation for craft ales which were a guarantee of quality on bars around the city.

Thankfully the Ridgeside story continues, though the two rock-inspired beers for which he was best known – the easy-going session pale **Jailbreak** (4%) and fulsome sweetish oatmeal stout **Black Night** (5%) – have now been retired, as brewers Matt Lovatt and James Newman turn their focus towards a broader range of styles.

The installation of a canning line into the space once occupied by the brewery tap was a key measure to get through Covid. "If we couldn't have sold cans we'd have struggled," says James, who joined the team a couple of years ago after a spell with Northern Monk at their vast new brewery in south Leeds.

"I wanted to be somewhere smaller, where I could have more of an influence over what we were brewing," he tells me over a beer in the new taproom, which opened in a neighbouring unit late in 2022. Here one cask and three keg lines – and fridges stocked with a host of alternatives – give drinkers the chance to taste the fruits of his labours.

The biggest seller is the hazy and sessionable dry-hopped pale ale **Objects in Space** (4.8%), whose fruit sharpness in the aroma soon dissolves into a soft and big-bodied lathering of the palate, with just the

Brewer James Newman

suggestion of some mandarin sweetness.

The anaemically-pale **You Can Be A Robot Too** (3%) may be a low-octane table beer, but still packs plenty of citric hop character, not least in an aroma bursting with pineapple. Jet-black **Larboard and Starboard** (5.9%) is an export porter of real distinction – full-bodied and with a pronounced chocolate aroma, but genuinely easy drinking with just a suggestion of dandelion and burdock and a drying finish.

Wild brett yeast lends significant influence on **Time Enough** IPA (6%) whose scrumpy bite combines with the piney notes of juniper berries in a complex tart taste. But, as can often happen, the palate soon acclimatises to this beer of sharpness and character.

The slightly stronger, creamy-banana-coloured **Green Greener** (6.3%) is nonetheless a more mainstream New Zealand IPA, not overly hoppy with some pronounced lime notes, and just a suggestion of parma violets. And it's surprisingly easy-drinking, as you briefly forget the strength and immerse yourself in a happy journey of antipodean discovery.

Ask The Birds (6%)

If a beer was to exemplify the adventurous spirit of today's Ridgeside it would be this deep amber saison, which brings the ancient techniques of the Wallonian farmhouse to a shiny brewkit in LS7. To create this sharply sour amber saison, the brewery's own yeast culture is blended with naturally-occuring yeast harvested in woodland nearby. "We set up yeast traps on Meanwood Ridge, and these became naturally inoculated with yeast from the air," explains James.

Beer brewed through spontanenous fermentation is notoriously unpredictable, but unlike in Belgium where they might blend different batches in order to assure some consistency, here it was a one-off – and, thankfully, it worked. Nelson Sauvin hops lend some fresh gooseberry to the flavour of a beer which seems quite shockingly sour at the first sip, though the palate soon adapts to its left-field assault. "It's an acquired taste," James admits. "But I was quite pleased with the results. There's a lot going on."

Riverhead Brewery

2 Peel Street, Marsden, Huddersfield, HD7 6BR; T: 01484 844324;
W: theriverheadmarsden.co.uk; E: brewery@ossett-brewery.co.uk;
f *@riverheadbrewerytap;* **𝕏** *@RiverheadBrewer*

Though now owned by regional heavyweight Ossett Brewery, Riverhead remains a tiny two-barrel plant whose production of just eight firkins a brew is largely swallowed wholesale by the brewery tap above. Brewer Richard Armitage produces an ever-changing catalogue of seasonal beers infused with locally-sourced fruits and herbs such as **Sherbert Lemon** (4.1%), in addition to his reservoir-themed regular beers, the assertive caramel and biscuity **March Haigh** (4.6%) and the full-bodied **Redbrook Premium** (5.5%). The **Cherry Stout** (4.3%) is an innovative take on this traditional style.

His best-known beer, the soothing, under-stated, lightly fruity, pale-copper **Butterley Bitter** (3.8%) is now produced back at the Ossett HQ, guaranteeing it the wider circulation it deserves.

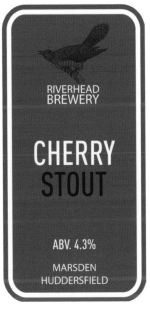

Rooster's Brewing Co

Unit H5, Fifth Avenue, Hornbeam Park, Harrogate, HG2 8QT; T: 01423 865959; W: roosters.co.uk; E: hello@roosters.co.uk; 🎵 🐦 📷 *@RoostersBrewCo*

Years from now, when someone traces the bloodline of the craft beer revolution, they will find Rooster's writ large in the DNA. Brewer Sean Franklin embraced the new hop varieties emerging in America's Yakima Valley, and put them front centre in a series of elegant, crisp, juicy pale ales.

It's not stretching a point too far to say that the sparkling spicy, floral, **Yankee** (4.3%) is a beer that turned the British brewing scene on its head. Now, it's a modern classic and relatively tame compared to some weightily-hopped newcomers, but they owe much to its bravery and ultimately its success. Still the brewery's flagship ale, it continues to pick up prizes, including a gold award at the 2022 SIBA North East Beer Competition.

Sean retired in 2011, and worked alongside twins Oliver and Tom Fozard to ensure a smooth transition to the new owners. Though they have substantially expanded the range, and invested heavily in increasing capacity, their beers remain true to Sean's legacy.

Rooster's stylish taproom looks out over the brewery

2019 saw a much-needed move to new premises in Harrogate. "This was all done so that we never have to move again," says Tom, over a beer in the former computer breaker's warehouse which became Rooster's new home in 2019. "Once a canning line had been installed at the Knaresborough brewery, the premises were practically full, and demand was such that we needed to start looking for somewhere bigger."

A 30-barrel brewery was built to Oliver's specifactions, while a second 10-barrel brewkit allows shorter-run beers including some which are going to barrel-ageing. Overlooking the brewery, an American-style taproom – albeit with both cask and keg beers – attracted a thirsty crowd from the neighbouring housing estates.

But then the pandemic arrived, forcing the brothers to switch production to canned beers, while they took advantage of the furlough scheme to retain their staff. It also spawned a new beer, the hazy American-style gluten-free pale ale **Thousand Yard Stare** (5.4%) whose name "reflects how battle weary we felt, as we didn't really know what the future of the brewery might look like," says Tom.

It was brighter than they might have thought, as loyal customers swamped their online shop with orders. "It was stressful, but heartwarming that people were willing to support us this way. It demonstrated that we have a really loyal following – and also gave us time to re-evaluate the range of beers." That included the launch of the crisp and golden lager-pale ale hybrid **Pilsnear** (4.8%) which has become the top-seller in a taproom which seats 160 and is often standing room only. It has been expanded with an events space upstairs and a sun trap beer garden for the summer.

The pandemic is now a fading memory: "It has given us confidence for the future," says Tom. "If we had still been in Knaresborough, we might not have survived. If we can come through that, we can come through anything."

This confidence is perhaps most evident in some of their limited edition beers. Bettys Cafe has been a much-loved Harrogate institution for a century. Their signature plump scones are the inspiration for **Scoundrel** (7.4%), described as a Fat Rascal pastry stout, and packed with cherry, lemon zest and just a suggestion of marzipan.

Oak barrels once used to mature Kentucky bourbon now lend their rich heritage to the imperial stout **Hello Dimitri** (11%), a warming, soothing, cherry brandy, marzipan syrup which I shared with revellers at a recent beer tasting in South Wales. It finishes with a sweet lathering of black treacle which clings to the back of the throat. "This would get right to a tickly cough," said one; "I'd love to try this in gravy," said another.

🍺 Baby-Faced Assassin (6.1%)

Rooster's reputation as a trendsetter didn't end with their enthusiastic adoption of American hops. In 2015 the brewery became one of the first in the UK to install its own canning line, a move once derided by the purists. There's a really enticing tropical fruit blast to the aroma of Baby Faced Assassin, one of the first three Rooster's beers given the aluminium treatment. This continues into a complex taste, heavy with mango and oranges, but so delightfully easy-drinking that its placid nature offers a false sense of security. Only when you read its strength in the small print do you realise the dangerous nature of this aptly-named assassin.

Rudgate Brewery

2 Centre Park, Marston Business Park, Tockwith, YO26 7QF;
T: 01423 358382; W: rudgatebrewery.co.uk; E: sales@rudgatebrewery.co.uk;
📘 🐦 📷 *@rudgatebrewery*

There's a whole heap of history here, from the Romans to the RAF. Marston Moor was the site of a pivotal civil war battle; 300 years later it was the wartime base for Halifax Bombers. In my youth, Tockwith was synonymous with learning to drive. Its old airfield has long been a place where learners can get behind the wheel, sure in the knowledge that there's nothing to crash into, other than long grass, traffic cones and, er, other learners.

Established in 1992 in the airfield's former ammunition store, the brewery is named after the old Roman road which crossed the Vale of York. **Ruby Mild** (4.4%) has some liquorice and toffee on the nose, then a big blast of ripe fruits on the palate, followed by a surge of unexpected late bitterness. The dark amber best bitter **Battleaxe** (4.2%) may lack the full-on thunderous potency suggested by the name, but has bags of damsonny, fruitloafy malt in the aroma and some nice caramel sweetness to the taste. **Valkyrie** (5%) is a nicely-constructed American pale ale, bursting with oranges and is again rather sweeter and more benign than its Wagnerian name suggests.

Covid spurred Rudgate on to establish its online shop. "This massively helped us to survive," says comms supremo Tiff Castle. Father's Day gift packs proved popular, and now on the other side of the pandemic, the brewery retains a strong customer base who order from their online shop.

Perhaps it was this underpinning strength which enabled Rudgate to emerge confidently from those dark times. 2022 saw a refreshed branding, and the launch of their first lagers, **Pilsnor** (4.7%) and the more sessionable **HUS** (4%). The pale ale **Opus** (4%) showcased the talents of the hop of the same name, and was created as part of a development programme spearheaded by hop merchants Charles Faram.

Rudgate love to freshen up their range with a cornucopia of seasonals, occasionals and specials; two new sessionable-strength ales are brewed

every month, to satisfy a thirst for a brewery which seems to go from strength to strength. That they now have Phil Marsh – the former driving force behind the much-missed Hungry Bear brewery – on board, is a further sign that they are heading in the right direction.

Jorvik (4.6%)

Jorvik, of course, is the Viking name for York, though it's unlikely the Scandinavian invaders had anything quite like this to drink. Styled a flaxen blond ale, this attractive golden beer with its prickly gingerish aroma is wonderfully refreshing, yet packed with the kind of fruit and marzipan flavours usually associated with darker, stronger, winter warmers.

And the truth is, if those Viking hordes had come across this stuff – or the slightly less potent cask version – they might have calmed down a bit and concentrated more on the simple pleasures of getting gently sozzled in like-minded company, rather than that whole strenuous and no doubt tiresome business of war, rape and pillage.

Ryedale Brewing

Roseberry, Moor Lane, Sinnington, York, YO62 6SE; T: 01751 433 229; W: ryedalebrewing.co.uk; E: info@ryedalebrewing.co.uk

After a spell brewing in Keighley, brothers David and Tony Williams are now back where they started in Ryedale – though I've struggled to find any of their beers in the preparation of this book. Hopefully this is just a small hiatus and we will soon see a welcome return for their core range of beers, including the pale golden **Angler** (3.8%), quintessential dark Yorkshire bitter **Rambler** (3.8%), and Chinook-driven **Ryedale Harvest** (3.8%).

SALT

199 Bingley Road, Saltaire, BD18 4DH; T: 01274 533848;
E: shop@saltbeerfactory.co.uk; W: saltbeerfactory.co.uk;
🅵 🅳 🅾 *@saltbeerfactory*

Mill owner Sir Titus Salt was reputedly teetotal. No pubs were allowed in the village he built for his workers, his dedication to a fervent non-conformism embodied in the beautiful canalside church opposite his mill where, incidentally, my dad was minister in the 1990s.

Whether the great philanthropist will be turning in his mausoleum about the village's growing brewery is open to question, but his high-minded non-conformist principles have long since been subsumed beneath a welter of fine public houses, notably Fanny's Alehouse, a short walk from the cobbled side streets of this UNESCO village.

The latest addition to the Ossett family of breweries and based in the village's former tram shed, SALT began with the simple dream of brewing great craft lager, but its scope evolved into something much greater. "We ventured out into the brewing world, equipped with only a single punchy vision – to make great craft beer for everyone and do it our way," says spokesperson Jess Mountford, warming to her theme.

"Tired of following tradition, we go where our brewing instincts take us, shamelessly combining heritage and modern brewery craft, crossing styles, exploring new ingredients and producing many award-winners along the way."

The taproom of this former tramshed features live music and woodfired pizzas – and from here the chain has expanded to four Leeds venues and to Boston Spa and London. As well as snaffling the old Leeds Brewery kit from Beeston, SALT has now opened a second brewery in Woolwich.

At each of these venues you can experience a growing range, which includes a sliding scale of IPAs: moderately bitter thirst-quencher **Jute** (4.2%), the more aggressively-hopped **Huckaback** (5.5%), dry-hopped and intensely tropical **Alpaca** (6.6%) and the intense, double dry-hopped, double IPA **Ikat** (8%).

A changing choice of stouts, lagers and brewing collaborations freshen the beer menu. The sessionable pale ale **Loom** (4%) is a recent addition. A distribution deal with Molson Coors takes the beers far and wide.

Jess ramps up the PR blurb yet further: "When it comes to crafting beer and pursuing our own evolution, we're pushing on at pace. We're growing, and so is our selection. There's now a whole world of great SALT craft beers just waiting for you to reach out and try. Don't thank us, like the beer, it's a pleasure."

And with a name like SALT, it's surely only a matter of time until they produce a Gose.

Saltaire Brewery

Dockfield Road, Shipley, Bradford, BD17 7AR; T: 01274 594959;
W: saltairebrewery.com; E: info@saltairebrewery.co.uk;
 @saltairebrewery

It remains a curiosity that Saltaire Brewery is a few hundred yards outside the World Heritage village, while SALT Brew Co is right at its heart. But the removal of Sir Titus Salt's great mill from their bottles and pump clips a few years ago represented an elegant distancing of themselves from the village: "We have a great reputation nationally and overseas," says boss Ewen Gordon. "Our beers go to 20 countries. Some drinkers know the village and its history, but for a lot of people Saltaire is simply the name of the brewery." Overseas sales have won for the brewery Export Champion accolades from Northern Powerhouse for four years in a row.

Based in an old generating station which once supplied the electricity for Bradford's trams, Saltaire has established itself as a regional powerhouse since brewing began 15 years ago. The design of their simple SB logo echoes the local street signs and the shallow sloping gable end of the tramshed's roofline.

Flagship beer **Saltaire Blonde** (4%) has some interesting sweet malty characteristics to balance its significant hoppy nature. Nelson Sauvin hops from New Zealand exert a muscular fruity influence to belie the moderate strength of **South Island** (3.5%), while the punchy, pithy **Cascade** (4.8%) features the bitter talents of the ubiquitous American hop.

The traditional bitter **Titus** (3.9%) pours an attractive copper colour with a firm and persistent creamy head that perhaps masks some of the aroma. But it really asserts itself on the palate, an insistent dry and grapefruit bitterness zings across the tongue, aided by some refreshing effervescence.

Creating an online business almost overnight helped Saltaire to ride out the pandemic by selling directly to customers online. During the long days

of lockdown, their delivery van became a familiar sight on my street, as several of my neighbours had clearly chosen Saltaire beers to help them dilute the miseries of Covid-19. Online sales remain buoyant now their pub and supermarket trade has been restored.

Perhaps encouraged by their continuing success, in 2020 Saltaire released its first lager, the crisp, clean, delicately hopped **Helles** (5%). This was followed by the light and refreshing **Pilsner** (4%), where the softness of the malt mingles beautifully with some subtle earthy spice to create a sessionable lager that stays true to its roots in old Bohemia, cradle of this classic style.

Whilst cask remains firmly at its core, a series of colourful cans are leading Saltaire's assault on the hipster end of the market. Of these, I particularly enjoyed the hazy, sunshine fruit expeience of **Zipwire** (4.5%), a zingy tangerine dream.

Triple Choc (4.8%)

The colour scheme used for this luxurious, indulgent stout echoes that of Cadbury's, as though the purple might elicit a Pavlovian response. It takes only a small shift in the balance of malts to effect a significant change of colour; here just 10% of chocolate malt is sufficient to ensure this beer emerges a seemingly impenetrable black. Only as you hold the glass to the light do you discern a little dazzle of ruby red. Its pale head clings with determination to the side of the glass as the level falls. There are some heady spirit-like influences on the nose, almost as though you have poured yourself a Baileys, and it shares some of the liqueur's indulgent creamy character on the palate. Some coffee and orange bitterness prevent the chocolate from being totally dominant.

Samuel Smith's

The Old Brewery, High Street, Tadcaster, North Yorkshire, LS24 9SB;
T: 01937 832225; W: samuelsmithsbrewery.co.uk;
🅵 📷 *@samuelsmithsbrewery* 🐦 *@ samsmithsbeer*

Fiercely, determinedly – sometimes maddeningly – traditional, Yorkshire's oldest brewery continues to plough its own distinctive furrow. The beers are brewed with water from the 85-foot well sunk in 1758, fermented in slate squares with the same strain of yeast they used in Victorian times, and delivered to their vast estate of pubs in wooden casks. When you step into one, whether in the north where there are many, or in London where there are several rather splendid ones, you are guaranteed only to find their own products – beers, wines, spirits, pop. Don't bother asking for the guest beer because they won't have one; don't use a mobile or you'll be booted out.

Head instead for the creamy and malty **Old Brewery Bitter** (4%), the lighter but dryer, hoppier **Best Bitter** (3.7%) or the robust caramelly **Dark Mild** (2.8%) whose bags of taste belie its shandy-level strength.

It's worth exploring their bottles too. Their fruit beers – Organic Cherry, Strawberry and Raspberry – are, like the idiosyncratic company itself, something of an oddity in brewing terms. Quite unlike the tart lambics of Belgian extraction, these soft and refreshing ales start life in Lincolnshire, where the ancient, time-warped All Saint's Brewery in Stamford produces a lovely handcrafted ale, which is shipped up the Great North Road to Tadcaster, where Sam Smith's blend this with organic fruit juice. **Organic Raspberry** (5.1%) is a surprising translucent red with a firm pink head, and the sweet aroma of fruit cordial; although the raspberries remain in evidence in the taste, they are never over-dominant.

During a year-long maturation in oak casks, **Yorkshire Stingo** (8%) develops the smooth, rounded dried-fruit and liquorice flavours which deftly disguise its strength. It delivers a rich and unexpected blast of

Sam Smith's is one of a handful of brewers which still use the traditional Yorkshire Square fermenting vessels.

The Old Brewery still employs a full-time cooper who makes and repairs all Samuel Smith's oak casks. These are used for handpulled Old Brewery Bitter and for maturing Yorkshire Stingo.

treacle as soon as it splashes across the tongue. Only in a long and genuinely warming aftertaste do you get a sense of its true potency.

Though brewed to a slightly different recipe each year, the sturdy seasonal ale **Winter Welcome** (6%) seems a high-octane take on the regular Sam Smith's Bitter – richer, maltier, more potent, and perhaps with some hints of brandy in the finish and a dry orangey aftertaste – its beautiful simplicity is emblematic of everything Tadcaster's wonderful, quirky, infuriating Old Brewery has been doing for generations.

Organic Chocolate Stout (5%)

This rich and sweetish luxurious dark ale comes in 550ml bottles, a characteristically perverse measure, 10 per cent more than half a litre, a splodge more than an American pint, and a splash short of an Imperial one. The label looks like something which might have been sent as a gift to troops in the Great War trenches. The chocolate – the product of organic chocolate malt and cocoa extract – announces itself from the moment you prise off the cap and its richness persists into the full-on luxury taste of a full-bodied beer. Some hints of vanilla emerge in a long sleepy finish.

Scarborough Brewery

Unit 21b, Barry's Lane, Scarborough, YO12 4HA;
T: 01723 367506; W: scarboroughbrewery.co.uk;
E: scarboroughbrews@gmail.com; 🅕 *@scarboroughbrewery*

2019 marked the tenth birthday of a brewery whose scallop shell logo and maritime beer names celebrate the resort's symbiosis with the sea. Lemon and passion fruit dominate the sessionable **Trident** (3.8%) and there is a significant fruity edge to the American-hopped golden ales **Sealord** (4.3%) and **Ship of Fools** (4.5%) which is given full voice in the toffee-and-tropical **Old Sailor** (4.9%).

There are some curious, perhaps slightly off-putting aromas to **Citra** (4.2%) but once on the palate its invigorating lemony flavours emerge, while a muscular **Stout** (4.6%) shifts the emphasis into coffee, chocolate, smoke, toast and prunes. Though of moderate strength, **Transmission** (3.9%) with its hoppy aroma and subtle citrus flavours is a perfect introduction to the range. Scarborough's Merchant Bar is the best place to find them.

Second Sight Brew Co

Halifax; W: secondsightbrew.co;
🅧 *@secondsightbrew;* 🅞 *@secondsightbrewco*

Currently cuckoo brewing while they search for their own premises in central Halifax, Second Sight is the brainchild of Chris Hall, a former brewer at Saltaire, and Simon Stather, owner of Halifax's Kobenhavn and the wonderfully atmospheric Victorian Craft Beer Cafe.

Their first brew was the aromatic session pale **Fairlight** (3.8%) produced in collaboration with Wishbone Brewery in Keighley. They then moved on to Turning Point in Knaresborough where they threw together a cocktail of five hops to create the hazy IPA **Just The Fax** (5.2%). A collaboration with Anthology in Leeds then led to the more sessionable IPA **Face the Fax** (4.3%).

Most recently, drinkers at the Victorian Beer Cafe's excellent Back In Black festival were wowed by the honey porter **Hive Mind** (4.3%), created with the help of Ilkley Brewery and a generous dose of locally-produced honey.

Selby (Middlebrough) Brewery

131 Millgate, Selby, YO8 3LL; T: 01757 702826;
E: martinsykesuk@yahoo.com

Companies House shows that this brewery was founded in 1945, but it ceased brewing in 1954 to concentrate on beer wholesaling and bottling Guinness.

And while its stylings still hark back to those gentler, happier, post-war years, the current incarnation only began life much more recently, when production was focused on servicing the nearby Howden Arms.

The sale of the pub will allow Selby's three cask beers – the pale ale **No.1** (4%), the traditional dark bitter **No.3** (4%) and the more substantial nutbrown **Old Tom** (6%) – to reach a wider audience at beer festivals and in free houses.

Settle Brewery

Unit 2B, The Sidings Ind Est, Settle, BD24 9RP; T: 01729 824936;
W: settle-brewery.co.uk; E: hops@settle-brewery.co.uk;
🅵 🅳 🅾 @settlebrewery

The Settle-Carlisle line offers one of the most spectacular rail journeys in Britain. From the sidings close to Settle station, the town's brewery is providing some similarly dazzling sensory experiences.

Its flagship craft products are the well-balanced and sessionable **Blonde** (3.6%) and the traditional Yorkshire ale **Ribblehead Bitter** (3.8%) whose energetic hop quality is balanced by some moderate dark fruit sweetness. **Attermire** (4.3%) is a proper juicy, citric IPA yet brewed to a mundane, sessionable strength; **Hoffman Gold** (4.1%) a crisp fruity refresher.

The creamy, coffee-ish **Ernie's Milk Stout** (4.5%) proved so popular it was promoted from the specials list to the core range.

Old Smithy Porter (4.7%) is a jet-black, creamy, smoky, coffee, caramel delight, while the seasonal American-influenced **Blood Orange IPA** (4.8%) demonstrates a thirst for the unusual.

Shadow Brewing

98 Boroughgate, Otley, LS21 1AE; T: 07792 690536;
W: www.shadowbrewing.co.uk; E: hello@shadowbrewing.co.uk;
🅕 *@shadowbrewing;* 🅣 🅘 *@shadow_brewing*

Ian Shutt established his one-barrel brewery at his home in 2019, after buying the bulk of his equipment from Wilde Child as Keir upgraded his own burgeoning operation. Four years on, and Shadow Brewing now has its own taproom in nearby Boroughgate, though the demands of Ian's day job have largely limited his regular opening times to Friday and Saturday evenings.

It's fast becoming a community hub: "We host a men's mental health group fortnightly on a Tuesday evening and a women's-only night on the last Wednesday of the month," says Ian. "Three book clubs use our space and we recently hosted English lessons for locally-based Ukrainian refugees." The community groups Otley 2030 and Wildlife Friendly Otley are others who have taken advantage of the space.

Those who find their way to the bar will usually be able to make acquaintance with at least two of Ian's brews. Along with the taproom itself, the bright and zesty sessionable pale ale **Phantom Signs** (3.6%), the firmer and more assertive American pale ale **Ghost** (4%) and the easy-drinking traditional IPA **Three Castles** (5%) are each evidence of a brewery emerging with confidence from the shadow of the pandemic.

Small World Beers

Unit 10, Barncliffe Business Park, Near Bank, Shelley,
West Yorkshire, HD8 8LU; T: 01484 602805;
W: smallworldbeers.com; E: info@smallworldbeers.com;
🅕 🅨 *@smallworldbeers*

The brewery's own borehole sources mineral water from the picturesque Barncliffe Valley, providing the liquor for a 20-barrel brewery established in 2013, which prides itself on deriving a high flavour profile from beers of relatively moderate strength.

They include the crisp, bright, full-flavoured **Long Moor Pale** (3.9%), the more noticeably sharp and hoppy **Spike's Gold** (4.4%) and the more full-bodied fruity pale **Twin Falls** (5.2%). The dry and toasty **Thunderbridge Stout** (5.2%), which draws its sweetness from chocolate malts, has garnered a string of awards.

A changing roster of seasonals and specials keeps things interesting; the golden **Winter Bank** (4%) develops surprising mango notes from its left-field hop combination.

Light citric **Eleven** (4%) is brewed for Remembrance Day with a donation from each pint sold going to the poppy appeal fund.

Another annual brew, the fresh green-hopped **Harvest Muse** (4%) uses hops picked in the early morning in the Midlands, before being rushed back north to ensure they are in the brew kettle within five hours.

A clutch of fine pubs in the rolling valleys between Huddersfield and Barnsley, such as the Tipsy Cow in Skelmanthorpe and George Inn in Upper Denby, each stock Small World beers.

 Barncliffe Bitter (3.7%)

I came across this beauty at the wonderful stone-built Woodman Inn at Thunderbridge, where the bar was packed with diners, while drinkers spilled out into a snowy beer garden on a crisp Sunday afternoon in March. This is a sturdy, full-bodied, modern take on a traditional Yorkshire bitter, rich and creamy on the palate and packed with orange, biscuit and apricot. Lovely.

St Mars of the Desert

90 Stevenson Rd, Sheffield, S9 3XG; T: 07365 222101; W: beerofsmod.co.uk;
E: brewery@beerofsmod.co.uk; 🅕 *@stmarsbrewery;* 🅣 🅘 *@beerofsmod*

Massachusetts' loss is Sheffield's gain. For eight years, brewers Dann
Paquette and Martha Holley-Paquette ran the Pretty Things Beer and Ale
Project in Boston, before relocating in 2018 to Sheffield. "We looked at
a lot of places to move to," says Dann, who has been brewing since the
1990s and is one of many to have Harrogate's Daleside Brewery on his CV.

"We almost decided on a village in Normandy called St Mars du
Desert, where we found a farm that was crying out to be a brewery." And
though the plans changed, the curious name stuck, and was eventually
appended to a couple of slightly ramshackle buildings east of Sheffield
city centre which were once part of a foundry where there is now an on-
site taproom for people to visit, tour, drink the beers and buy bottles to
take away.

In addition to four conical fermentation vessels and a range of wooden
vessels including 1,000-litre sherry butts and a 1,200-litre oak foeder,
the brewery includes a koelschip – one
of very few in the UK. Pronounced
'coolship', these broad shallow
vessels are used in the production of
wild beers, as in the lambic process
in Belgium. However at St Mars the
koelschip is used in a more traditional
way, in common with most traditional
German lager breweries, to cool and
add hop flavour and aroma to the
beer post-boil and pre-fermentation.

Dann Paquette

Though small in size, St Mars (or SMOD to its friends), produces a vast and diverse range: traditional lagers of all colours, others marked by their smokiness or hoppiness, sour and wild beers, big dark stouts, Belgian Abbey-type beers and a bottle refermented range. Its well-known koelschip IPA series includes the hazy golden **Clamp** (5.4%), whose blend of Waimea and Mosaic hops lend citrus, sweet fruit and stone fruit aromas before some zesty bitterness takes over at the finish.

When I first tried it at Sheffield Indie Beer Feast in 2023, the golden **Dormouse** (5.5%) seemed a curious aberration, though the palate soon acclimatised to its unique blue cheese assault.

🍺 **Lupé** (5.5%)

From a sweet-scented aroma right through to a booming bitter aftertaste, juicy Mandarina hops from Bavaria punch their significant weight in this full-bodied hazy golden ale. There's some toffee there too, and a tart marmalade bitterness to a beer of premium strength which is dangerously easy to drink.

Stancill Brewery

Unit 2, Oakham Drive, Sheffield, S3 9QX; T: 0114 2752788;
W: stancillbrewery.co.uk; E: tom@stancillbrewery.co.uk;
f 🐦 📷 *@stancillbrewery*

When lifelong friends Tom Gill and Adam Hague salvaged brewing kit from the closed down Oakwell Brewery in 2013, they persuaded Oakwell's head brewer Jonny Stancill to join them at the new venture in Sheffield – and they even put his name over the door.

Soft Peak District spring water goes into the production of a range of ales of sessionable strength, which is augmented by specials released monthly. The core range has long included the light and floral **Stainless** (4.3%), malty traditional English pale ale **No 7** (4.3%) and the soft, golden, refreshing **Blonde** (3.9%).

Crisp, clean **Sheffield Pilsner** (5%) is brewed with hops from Germany and the Czech Republic, and quad-filtered for authentic Central European clarity, while gentle pale ale **Elsie-May** (4%) celebrated a new arrival to the Stancill family. Seasonal alternatives include a sessionable stout, the nutty, creamy **Stancill Black** (3.7%) and the dark toffee-ish refresher **Porter** (4.4%).

"Thankfully the brewery is somehow still here post-Covid," says brewery spokesperson Hannah Gill. "But the after-shocks are still being felt in terms of supply chain and rising production costs, as I am sure they are in many other small businesses."

Even so, Stancill seem intent on developing their products. A new range of vegan craft keg beers comprises the refreshing ginger ale **Roxie** (4.2%), dry-hopped IPA **Amazona** (5%) and the mightily-hopped **Komrade** (6%), the strongest beer yet to emerge from the Stancill brewkit. Their 'Straight From The Tank' concept – basically 'rough beer' which has not been touched or fined between tank and cask – is a further exciting development.

Their two pubs, The Closed Shop in Commonside and The Albion on London Road serve exclusively Stancill beers, which are also farmed out to pubs in Yorkshire, Nottinghamshire, Derbyshire and beyond. For home drinkers, the bottled beers they sold for the first time as a stop-gap during the pandemic may return soon in response to sustained demand.

Barnsley Bitter (3.8%)

For a beer of such uncomplicated beauty, the history of Barnsley Bitter is a surprisingly complex one. In the immediate post-war years, Barnsley Bitter's popularity grew from the mining communities of south Yorkshire to become a national phenomenon, eulogised by celebrity locals such as Parky and Dickie Bird.

In the seventies, Barnsley Brewery was taken over by Courage and closed down, before Oakwell Brewery started brewing a version in the 1990s from a unit on the same site. Also during the late nineties another Barnsley Bitter was being brewed in Elsecar, though the brewery closed and production was switched to Blackpool Brewery – a move unlikely to find favour in Yorkshire. Meanwhile, Dave Hughes, who had been head brewer at Elsecar, set up Acorn brewery, whose own Barnsley Bitter has now become a local favourite.

Oakwell closed in 2013, paving the way for the establishment of Stancill's renascent dark amber ale with its nicely-rounded malt and caramel character which was immediately named Champion Beer of Yorkshire.

Steel City Brewing

The Circle, 33 Rockingham Lane, Sheffield, S1 4FW;
W: www.facebook.com/groups/140082354063/;
E: dave.unpronounceable@gmail.com; @steelcitybrewing

Though it's now common practice, Steel City were among the UK's first cuckoo brewers – holding their own licence but creating their beers on other brewers' kit. Headed by self-styled Dave Unpronounceable, Steel City was set up to address a perceived lack of truly hoppy beers available in the UK: "That now seems ridiculous, with a nuclear arms race of hops going on," he says.

Steel City remains a cuckoo in Lost Industry's nest, brewing irregular one-off beers, most likely to be found at Shakespeare's, The Rutland and The Crow in Sheffield. The two breweries regularly work together, as well as collaborating with other brewers from near and far; their original hop-heavy output is now interspersed with imperial stouts, sours – and the enthusiastic adoption of barrel-ageing.

Stod Fold Brewing

Ogden, Halifax, HX2 8XL; T: 01422 245951; W: stodfoldbrewing.com;
E: Paul@stodfoldbrewing.com; 🅕 🅣 *@stodfold;* 🅸 *@stodfolddeanclough*

Given how its reputation has spread, it's surprising to learn that Stod Fold has only been around since 2015. Its core ales have already gained quite a following, with distribution across around 300 individual free trade outlets, predominantly in Yorkshire. These include the simple refreshing **Gold** (3.8%), the dark brown roasty **Dark Porter** (4.8%) and the smooth **Blonde+** (4.3%), which uses a different blend of hops with each brew.

The acidic aromas of the new **West American Pale** (4%) persist into a light-as-a-feather fruit cocktail on the palate, ending in a crisp dry finish.

Brewer and co-owner Paul Harris is namechecked in the amber-coloured traditional English IPA **Dr Harris** (5.7%) which has some floral notes and deep earthy character.

In April 2022, Stod Fold unveiled two limited edition ales to commemorate the 231st birthday of Anne Lister, made famous through the TV series *Gentleman Jack* written by the local dramatist and scriptwriter Sally Wainwright OBE.

Anne Lister's Dark (4.8%) is a velvet porter; her lover is immortalised in the refreshing pale **Ann Walker's Blonde** (4.3%).

Seasonal beers such as the substantial, oat-fortified **Rum Porter** (5.5%) flesh out the range; the well-established brewery tap in Halifax's artsy Dean Clough centre is the best place to enquire after the latest.

Stubbee Brewery *New*

22 Harry Street, Dudley Hill, Bradford, BD4 9PH; T: 01274 933444;
W: stubbee.co; 🅕 🅘 *@stubbee.co;* 🅣 *@stubbee*

By the time Salamander brewery appeared in the first edition of this book
in 2017, it had already been going for almost 20 years – and brewer Dan
Gent had won a string of awards for his beers. Yet by the second edition,
just two years later, they were no more.

And there the story might have ended, had Dan not struck up a
friendship with Aussie Allen McKenna. They bonded over a love of beer
and revived the brewery as Stubbee – the familiar Australian name for a
small beer bottle.

Dan lends an approximation of his name to the hop-forward session ale
Darn Genet (3.8%) and there are some spicy notes both to the session
bitter **Dead River** (4%) and the Christmas special **Brewdolph** (3.8%)

As well as these newcomers, it made perfect business sense to revive
some of Dan's much-loved Salamander recipes such as the copper-
coloured, fruity best bitter **Mudpuppy** (4.2%) and the refreshingly
grapefruity **Golden Salamander** (4.5%), a former silver medallist at the
Great British Beer Festival.

Long Reign IPA (5.2%) was produced for the Queen's platinum jubilee
celebrations in 2022 – and as this third edition of the book went to press,

Allen and Dan were hard at work on a special brew for King Charles's coronation.

And they are investing in the future, with an expanded brewkit due to come fully onstream later in 2023 and a new bottling plant which will allow them to extend their list of bottled beers beyond the core Salamander range. A taproom opens each Friday evening to allow customers to drink the produce on the premises.

Stubbee are big supporters of local sport, and have sponsorship deals with both Bradford Bulls and Bradford Park Avenue, as the bars at the stadiums bring a new and thirsty clientele for these gloriously revitalised beers.

Platypus Porter (4.8%)

Like the other Stubbee bottled beers, this rich dark ale retains the Salamander branding. It's described as a 'full flavoured porter' on the label, which begs the question what a half-flavoured one might taste like. No matter, it doesn't disappoint. There are some interesting yeasty, bready aromas as you prise off the lid, but these give way to some lightly vinous flavours, some tobacco and the softness of damsons on the palate, before it departs with smoky notes in the long finish.

Sunbeam Ales

52 Fernbank Road, LS13 1BU; T: 07772 002437; W: sunbeamales.co.uk; E: nigelpoustie@yahoo.co.uk; 🗗 🖸 🖾 *@SunbeamAles.*

Had brewer Nigel Postie made his home in one of Leeds's less evocatively-named streets – South Accommodation Road or Grimthorpe Avenue maybe – he would probably have found a different way of naming his brewery. But when you live in Sunbeam Terrace and brew the beers in your garage, you may as well celebrate the address – even after you have decamped to LS13. He further honours the location with the zesty **Born in LS11** (5.1%), one of his most popular ales.

Nigel brews once a week, occasionally twice, rotating through a range of beers and some occasional seasonals. They include juicy tropical fruit IPA **Sun Kissed** (3.7%) and coffee-and-orange-peel-infused stout **Eclipse** (3.8%). First brewed as a 'bag-in-a-box' ale for home drinking during lockdown, the enticingly-named **Black Forest Gateau Porter**

(4.8%) has remained part of the range.

Nigel's **Chocolate Mild** (4.8%) is a former winner at Calderdale beer festival; its **White Chocolate Mild** stablemate (4.2%) a pre-pandemic beer of the festival at Bradford.

The Beehive in Shipley has now given a permanent place to **Nigel's Plum Porter** (4.8%), while **Polka Hop Pale** (3.8%), golden bitter **Bright Day** (4.2%) and session pale **Bottoms Up** (3.7%) are now the house beers at Wakefield's Polka Hop, Bradford's Jacob's, and Oscars in Morley respectively.

Changeable (4.2%)
The stylised sunset of the Sunbeam Ales pump clip forms an eye-catching image wherever it can be found. Changeable is so named because it uses a different hop variety in each iteration of the brew. This one – bright gold, smooth, and with a firm crisp bite soon giving way to a compassionate blanketing of malt – showcases the talents of Summit, and those of Nigel himself.

Talking Tides *New*

86, Greenlands Road, Redcar, TS10 2DH; E: Beer@talkingtides.com;
W: www.talkingtides.com; ⓕ @Talking-Tides-Brew-Co; ⓧ ⓘ talkingtides

A random set of fortunate events led to Ste, Pete and Josh meeting each other in 2021 – and apparently the brewery was born in minutes. The Signals cafe and taproom in Saltburn saw the launch of their first two beers, and both soon sold out. Though Talking Tides remains a part-time venture for all of them, their beers have already crossed the country to reach retailers in Manchester, and crossed the North Sea to Amsterdam.

Tapped Brew Co

Sheffield Station, Sheaf St, Sheffield, S1 2BP; T: 0114 273 7558; and 51 Boar Lane, Leeds, LS1 5EL; T: 0113 2441953;
W: tappedbrewco.com; E: info@tappedbrewco.com; ⓕ ⓧ @tappedbrewco

For more than ten years, Tapped Brew Co has been brewing in the beautiful surroundings of Sheffield's Edwardian first-class refreshment rooms. The four-barrel brewkit is in full view, allowing customers to drink while watching the brewers at work. The session IPA **Sheaf Street** (4.5%) really showcases the talents of Mosaic and Centennial hops, with its aromas of pineapple and mango and the more bitter nature of grapefruit in the taste, in a beautifully-balanced, sessionable pale. Others in the range include **Cannon** (4.2%) – surely a nod to the local favourite Stones – a traditional best bitter, and **Sorsby** (4%) a dry stout. Further station taps have followed in York, Harrogate and at Euston – while a second brewery in Boar Lane, Leeds, adds keg ales to the cask beers brewed in Sheffield.

Tarn 51 Brewing

Robin Hood, 10 Church Road, Altofts, WF6 2NJ; T: 01924 892911;
W: tarn51brewing.co.uk; E: realale@tarn51brewing.co.uk;
ⓕ ⓧ @tarn51brewing

The Robin Hood, a former Wakefield CAMRA pub of the year, is the place to sample the produce from Tarn 51's three-barrel brewery next door. The two core beers are the crisp **Altofts Blonde** (4%) and the easy going **Birkwood Bitter** (3.9%), with specials often including a pale and a stout.

Tartarus 🥚New🥚

Unit 6, Taverner's Walk Industrial Estate, Sheepscar, Leeds, LS7 1AH;
W: www.tartarusbeers.co.uk; E: tartarus.brewing@gmail.com;
🇫 🇩 📷 @tartarusbeers

The bewildering expansion of North Bar group opened the way for this bright newcomer to the Leeds scene.

North's brewery was based in Sheepscar from 2015 before relocating to vast new premises nearby during the pandemic while Jack Roberts and Jordan Orpen juggled full-time jobs with brewing in their Horsforth cellar.

"We wanted to call the brewery Elysium, the Greek word for heaven," says Jack, who brings his love of mythology to the names of the beers. "There was already a brewery called that so we went for the opposite – Tartarus is the Greek hell."

Furlough from Brew York gave Jack the opportunity to take Tartarus to the next level, first as cuckoo brewers with Legitimate Industries and then by inheriting North's Taverner's Walk site just outside the city centre. "We'd been putting out feelers for about 18 months, trying to find somewhere, before we were contacted by North."

Having their own brewery has allowed Tartarus to scale production up to around 5,000 litres a fortnight, bring their packaging in-house and serve beers in their very own taproom, which opened in November 2022. This is certainly the most reliable place to find them; though wholesalers take their cans and kegs far and wide, Tartarus has yet to really crack the local market. "It seems quite cliquey in Leeds," says Jack. "We've been in Friends of Ham and Brownhills, but a lot of the bars seem to use the same breweries time after time."

So an evening in a taproom lined by huge conical fermenting vessels and decorated simply by festoons of bare bulbs and strings of beer can labels, allowed us to commune with the Tartarus pantheon. The Chinese interpret lunar markings as a **Moon Rabbit** (0.5%) and this seemed like a great place to start; a low-alcohol stout which still packs in bags of rich coffee and vanilla. A mythical German woodland creature lends its name to the sweetish helles **Wolpertinger** (4%) while the grapefruity cloudy pale **Ratotskr** (4.4%) honours a Norse messenger squirrel. There was just a suggestion of tarmac to our ride with the blackberry-accented black IPA **Valkyrie** (6.2%), perhaps the one slightly missed step of our evening's drinking.

A pair of spicy pales honour hobgoblins, one French, one German. The first, **Lutin** (4.5%) is a dry-hopped saison alive with cloves and toffee with grassy overtones and these flavours are given full voice in the easy-going

Jordan Orpen and Jack Roberts

yeasty, spicy hefeweizen **Kobold** (5.5%).

From here the strengths spiral upwards to the Gods – and while we couldn't try them all, we did leave room for the bewitching **Abaddon** (17%) comfortably the strongest beer I've ever tried. Appropriately named for the biblical angel of the abyss, this is black as Whitby jet, with a devilish cocoa aroma, and a complex, mouth-filling, sense-numbing taste of hazelnut, espresso, Tia Maria, Baileys, and all the dangerous flavours of temptation. It's brutal, but beautiful too.

 Snawfus (4.5%)

Named for a winged deer of America's Ozark Mountains this was the best of a rather wonderful bunch. There are some piney notes in the aroma, which linger into a chunky, grainy, fruity tasting beer, where the hops are given full rein, but beautifully balanced by a significant malt presence. From its pale copper colour, through to its assertive finish, this is almost a traditional Yorkshire bitter, but with bags of characteristic Tartarus attitude.

Theakston Brewery

The Brewery, Masham, Ripon, HG4 4YD; T: 01765 680000;
W: theakstons.co.uk; E: info@theakstons.co.uk;
🅕 🅧 @Theakston1827; 🅞 @theakstonbrewery

Visitors are welcomed daily to Robert Theakston's tower brewery – the third site used for brewing since it began in 1827. Beer has been in constant production here since 1875; all of it passes through the original Victorian mash tun. One copper vessel is a relatively new addition, having been installed in 1936, though it was second-hand, even then.

Perhaps more than any other brewery in Yorkshire, Theakston maintain and preserve the county's oldest brewing traditions. The appointment of Simon Theakston to the ceremonial role of Master of the ancient Worshipful Company of Brewers in 2019 was recognition of the brewery's long and proud contribution to the industry. And when new cooper Euan Findlay ended his four-year apprenticeship in 2021, he was trussed up in a 54-gallon hogshead and rolled around the brewery yard in an initiation dating back to Chaucer's times.

These vast barrels lend their name to **Hogshead Bitter** (4.1%), one of the brewery's range of seasonal ales. Ruby-brown, with a gentle effervescence and suggestions of coffee, toffee and dark cherries, it packs more mature fruit taste and character into its very moderate bandwidth than some brewers manage in far stronger ales.

Theakston beers are widely available across the county, particularly across the Dales and north Yorkshire. **Best Bitter** (3.8%) is a quintessential Yorkshire ale; bright and golden **Lightfoot** (4.1%) has soothing peachy flavours, while late hopping with Golding hops gives **Black Bull** (3.9%) a pronounced hoppy edge. Keg, craft keg and a host of seasonals fill out the roster, among them the lovely unpasteurised and cold-filtered **Barista Stout** (4.2%).

Theakston and neighbours Black Sheep remain fierce rivals, not least because of the bloodline which connects the two family-owned brewers.

Old Peculier (5.6%)

Sales of some big-name beers are suffering in an over-crowded marketplace, yet those with the history and cachet of Old Peculier will comfortably survive. The words "The Legend" on the label are fully justified. From its peculiar spelling to the town's seal of a crimson-clad Roger de Mowbray kneeling in apparent supplication, Theakston Old Peculier is every inch a Yorkshire legend.

This deep red-brown ale has less of a significant aroma than you might expect from a beer of this strength, yet it more than compensates with a full-on assault on the palate. Smooth and full-bodied, it blends rich, dried fruit, Christmas cake flavours with the woody, grainy, almost nutty nature of the malts and caramels and just a suggestion of black pepper, which persists into a long aftertaste that develops sufficient bitterness to make you eager to down still more. To taste it is to commune with history.

Three Fiends Brewhouse

Brookfield Farm, Mill Moor Road, Meltham, Holmfirth, HD9 5LN; T: 07810 370430; W: threefiends.co.uk; E: sales@threefiends.co.uk; ☐ threefiendsbrewhouse; ☐ ☐ @threefiends

The fiendish trio who set up this brewery in 2015 have been friends since they met at school aged 11. They scored an early success when spicy and distinctly orangey **Bad Uncle Barry** pale ale (4.2%) was named Best Bitter at Huddersfield's Oktoberfest in 2016. Now slimmed down to a duo, the last few years have seen their expansion to a 10-barrel plant and the opening of a taproom. A horsebox repurposed as a mobile bar allows them to spread the word further afield.

The beer range has also been overhauled, while fresh designs have created a bold new look. Choices now include the big-tasting citrus NEIPA **Bandito** (4.5%) and the more challenging, dank and piney West Coast **Super Sharp Shooter** (5.2%).

Perfectly named, the craft IPA **Two Face** (4%) offers two contrasting flavour experiences. It presents with an effervescent aroma rich with zesty, fruity notes – but then hits the palate with a surprisingly firm, decisive, almost aggressive dry bitterness. And all this from an ale of such moderate, delicate strength. If there's some two-faced drinking

acquaintance who you feel might deserve a taste of their own medicine, this could be just the thing.

Their Fourth Fiend taproom in Meltham – a wonderful re-use of the local Conservative Club, whose name remains in its ornate stained glass – is the perfect place to try the range.

Stelfox (4%)

Most New England IPAs are on the strong side, not least Three Fiends' own piney tropical **Punch Drunk** (5.5%). Of those featured in this edition, most are north of 5%, with many pushing several percentage points higher. So it's a refreshing change to encounter a genuinely sessionable interpretation of this most fashionable of styles. And what Stelfox may lack in full-on potency, it compensates for with a really rich and complex flavour experience. There are some lemony, grassy notes to the aroma, which are blown away by a fanfare of sunshine fruit on the palate – mango, tangerine and white grapes – before some woody, earthy notes emerge in the finish. It's so fiendishly good that I'm not sure it's worth migrating to the 7.5% version **Stelfoxed** which concentrates the experience yet further.

Tigertops Brewery

22 Oakes Street, Flanshaw, Wakefield,
WF2 9LN; T: 01924 897728;
E: tigertopsbrewery@hotmail.com;
W: www.tigertopsbrewery.co.uk;
 f *@TigertopsBreweryWakefield*

One website lists over 230 different brews created by this innovative
brewery, which was established by Stewart and Lynda Johnson, now of
the Prince of Wales brewpub at Foxfield in Cumbria. Their friend Barry
Smith is now the brewer; his day job cutting trees and verges for the
local council has earned him the nickname Axeman. Barry's taste for the
continental is illustrated by beers such as the wheat beers **White Max**
(4.6%) and **Blanche de Newland** (4.5%), but **Alverthorpe Atom** porter
(4.8%) and traditional bitter **Flanshaw Flyer** (4.4%) place him solidly
back in the WF postcodes. The range is expanding all the time.

Timothy Taylor's

Knowle Spring Brewery, Keighley, BD21 1AW; T: 01535 603139;
W: timothytaylor.co.uk; E: tim@timtaylors.co.uk;
 f 🐦 *@timothytaylors;* 📷 *@timothytaylorsbrewery*

Timothy Taylor's long commitment to cask ale and great pubs was
marked in 2021 by a CAMRA Golden Award, as part of the campaign
group's 50th anniversary celebrations. A further award in 2022 – UK's
Best Independent Craft Brewery Webshop at the SIBA Business Awards
– recognised the efforts they had made to emerge unscathed from a
pandemic where bottle sales and personalised glassware maintained their
steady momentum.

A swathe of new beers to sit alongside Taylor's time-honoured products
has seen head brewer Andy Leman give his own gently-modernising
stamp to the brewery. These include the caramel and chocolate-
rich **Poulter's Porter** (4.8%) and aromatic **Hopical Storm** (4%), the
brewery's first permanently-available kegged ale. Three stages of hopping
with whole-leaf British hops lend a real depth of flavour, with suggestions
of mandarin, mango and passion fruit.

But the brewery's success is underpinned by the phenomenal success
story of Taylor's core beers, which include the beautifully-balanced,
sessionable **Boltmaker** (4%), sweet and toffee-ish **Dark Mild** (3.5%) and
zesty and palate-cleansing **Golden Best** (3.5%).

Why our yeast needs to be locked up

You might well wonder why we lock away our yeast. Until you learn how important it is to the flavour of our beer. We use our own unique strain called, appropriately, *Taylor's Taste*. The properties of this particular yeast are vital to giving Landlord its deep and complex yet crisp and clean flavour. It's so valuable to us that every year two samples of Taylor's Taste are carefully transported to separate secret locations and stored carefully under lock and key, just in case the precious yeast here at the brewery is ever compromised or damaged. It might seem over cautious, but it's *all for that taste of Taylor's.*

All for that taste of Taylor's

The easy-going mild ale **Landlord Dark** (4.3%) – formerly known as Ram Tam – bathes the palate in gentle treacle and caramel; amiable orange-and-spice refresher **Knowle Spring Blonde** (4.2%) is named after the artesian well which provides the water for all the Taylor beers. Oaty, warming **Havercake Ale** (4.7%), released around Armistice Day, honours the West Riding's links to the Duke of Wellington's Regiment with 10p from every sale now going to soldiers' charity ABF.

Which is all to say nothing of the iconic **Landlord** (4.3% cask, 4.1% bottle), a global phenomenon which has been Champion Beer of Britain four times and runner-up on three occasions. No other ale can come close to that record; few others can claim to have been championed by Madonna.

But the new broom has swept even here, with the label's avuncular red-waistcoated licensee supplanted by his slightly chiselled great-nephew. Yet Landlord continues to look as lovely as ever – bright amber with a tight white head that releases an enticing aroma born of the cocktail of three hops thrown into the time-honoured brew. There's an earthy, bitter, marmalade nature to the taste, delicately balanced by suggestions of apple and toffee malt before this full-bodied beer dies away in a long and slightly sweet finish.

By its name, its recipe, its brewery, its design and its history, Timothy Taylor's Landlord is an absolute national treasure. It is England's greatest county distilled into a pint of perfection.

Half a mile from the brewery, the new taproom and kitchen Taylor's

On The Green is the ideal place to immerse yourself in this whole joyous Timmy Taylor's experience.

 Cook Lane IPA (5.8%)

If this is Andy's attempt to muscle in on the hipster markets of craft ale, then its low-key labelling ensures it remains a subtle one, entirely in keeping with a brewery so anchored to its traditions. Cook Lane references the brewery's original Victorian home, and is a fitting name for a beer which takes India Pale Ale back to its roots as an English ale, packed with home-grown ingredients. Aromatic Cascade and Chinook hops lend significant aroma to a big-bodied, bright golden ale which has a slightly oily feel on the palate, some bitter orange marmalade flavours and a crunchy Daim Bar finish. Andy's signature gives his personal imprimatur to a beer which demonstrates his determination to put his own stamp on Taylor's long and proud history.

Toolmakers Brewery

6-8 Botsford Street, Sheffield, S3 9PF; T: 01142 454374;
W: toolmakersbrewery.com; E: info@toolmakersbrewery.com;
🐦 @toolmbrewery; 📷 @toolmakersbrewery

The toolmaking theme is entirely appropriate to an area steeped in steelmaking, and a whole host of beers build on that theme. Munich malt adds some caramel to **Lynch Pin** (4%), while **Slip Joint** (4%) is a softly spoken traditional bitter. **Black Edge** (5.2%) is a deep roasty, malty stout. The on-site bar is both a brewery tap and a party venue available for hire, while the Forest Bar in Rutland Street provides a further ready route to market.

Alex Barlow gets the beers in at Triple Point

Triple Point Brewing

178 Shoreham St, Sheffield, S1 4SQ; T: 07828 131423;
W: triplepointbrewing.co.uk; E: alex@triplepoint.beer; 🅵 🅾 *@triplepointbrew*

The task of scratching off the Sentinel Brewery branding from the distinctive curvy glassware was just one which had to be completed before this city-centre taproom re-opened as Triple Point in March 2019 after a long and painful hiatus. "Sentinel was great, but it cost so much to run, it wasn't sustainable," says former boss Alex Barlow, who remains as Head Brewer following a period of administration and re-structuring which saw a change of ownership and a new management team. "I was a reluctant boss anyway. First and foremost I'm a brewer, and I didn't want to be doing everything else that a boss has to do."

The Triple Point name references the 'Science, Art and Magic' of brewing. "The science is our core range, the art is about trial beers and new techniques, the magic is what will come from collaborating with other brewers," Alex explains.

Sheffield's Indie Beer Feast in March 2023, offered a welcome opportunity to acquaint myself with some of his new range, like the lovely dry and citric pale **Cirrus** (5%) and the beautifully-summery **Trio** (3.8%)

whose fruit basket of lemon and lime is derived from a trio of hops – citra, mosaic and amarillo. **Mochacao** (7.8%) is a firm and assertive chocolate and coffee stout, **Cryo** (4.2%) an intensely hoppy pale.

Alex's love of lager is indulged by the crisp **Helles**, (4.1%), yeasty, substantial **Vienna** (4.9%) and – best of all – the golden, clear, crisp, slightly limey Dortmund-style **Konig** (5.3%).

Recently expanded, the on-site taproom is the ideal place to try this revamped range. Here, a high corrugated roof, painted brickwork and factory lighting embrace the building's industrial purpose, re-positioning it for social use. High glass windows divide drinkers from the steel brewing vessels and fermenting tanks while taps on the bar are primed with all the latest produce.

True North Brew Co

127-129 Devonshire Street, Sheffield, S3 7SB; T: 0114 272 0569;
W: truenorthbrewco.uk; E: bookings@truenorthbrewco.uk;
🅵 🅳 *@truenorthbrewco*

True North grew from a long-standing venues venture, adding beer, gin and vodka production businesses along the way, and bringing them under a single name in 2016.

Around the same time they stepped up from being cuckoo brewers at Welbeck Abbey in Nottinghamshire to using their own city-centre brewhouse. From here, head brewer Dean Hollingworth supplies the group's own 11 pubs, as well as other independent venues.

Czech Saaz and Tetnanger hops lend a crispness to the **Sheffield Pilsner** (5%), while Amarillo and Simcoe bring their fruity, piney characteristics to the pale **Polaris** (4.3%). **Blonde** (4%) is golden, floral-scented and vanilla-accented, sessionable **Best Bitter** (3.8%) a no-nonsense brown ale which taps into the traditional end of the market.

A recent partnership with giants Molson Coors has allowed True North to bring a famous name back to the city. **Stones Bitter** (4.1%) was first produced in 1948 – and is famous for its long-running TV ad campaigns. Now Dean has been given access to the beer's original cask recipe and has breathed new life into a brand that is Sheffield to its core.

Truth Hurts Brew Co

City Mills, Peel Street, Morley,
West Yorkshire, England LS27 8QL;
E: paul@truthhurts.co.uk;
 @truthhurtsbrew;
 @truthhurtsbrewery

A switch to off-sales allowed Truth Hurts to ride out the pandemic by selling bag-in-box and minikeg versions of their beers. This success is testament to the impact they made – with beers such as the determinedly bitter **Part Time Punk**

IPA (5.8%) and the tangy pale ale **King Kiwi** (6%) – in the short time between establishing the brewery in 2018 and the arrival of Covid a little more than a year later. Now on the other side, they have developed their Beer Thirty bottle shop into a taproom, selling more of their own beer fresh in keg and cask.

They have also extended the range through the creamy, powerful **Double Molotov Milkshake** (8.5%) and some fruitful collaborations with the likes of Raven Hill and Radiant breweries.

Turning Point Brew Co

Unit 3, Grimbald Park Industrial Estate, Wetherby Road,
Knaresborough, HG5 8LJ; T: 01423 869967;
W: turningpointbrewco.com; E: info@turningpointbrewco.com;
🅵 🅸 *@turningpointbrewco;* 🅓 *@turningpointbco*

Founded in 2017 in Kirkbymoorside, Turning Point had
gathered sufficient momentum to move into bigger
premises vacated by Rooster's in Knaresborough just two
years later.

The funky, juicy American pale ale **Disco King** (5.1%)
is their only core beer, though a host of others, from the
light and sessionable **Radio Nowhere** pale (3.8%) to
the fulsome rich and sweet **The Second Law** (12%) are
available in cans, from the brewery taproom and at their
other venues, The Outpost and The Falcon
in York.

The breadth of their output indicates
that brewers Aron and Cameron are
keen to experiment. Autumn ale **Night
Must Fall** (5.3%) is a blackberry sour further
enriched by damson and lemon balm; **Chaos Theory**
(5%) derives its warm and earthy flavour from honey
and marigold, while oatmeal lends extra body.

🍺 **Magnificent Gestures** (6.5%)

The dramatic label, somewhere between a Turner
masterpiece and a prog rock album cover, drew
me to this one at the fine bottle shop Bier Huis in
Ossett. This rich, full, big-bodied, juicy New England
IPA pours a murky pale with an exaggerated foaming
white head, which releases some enticing tinned
peach aromas. These lead on to a complex bitter fruit
taste with apples and white wine loaded onto bags of
citrus, all the product of its citra, ekuamot and simcoe
hop cocktail. Its dry finish leaves a warming calling
card on the back of the throat.

Vocation Brewery

8 Craggs Country Business Park, Cragg Vale, Hebden Bridge, HX7 5TT;
T: 01422 410810; W: vocationbrewery.com; E: sales@vocationbrewery.com;
🄵 🄳 *@vocationbrewery*

"It's all been pretty mental," says brewing director Matt Howgate over an afternoon coffee in Vocation's hilltop brewery high above Hebden Bridge. "I've been here since 2018 and it's been a time of rapid expansion. We went from 8,000 hectolitres, to 13, to 25, and now to 60."

When it was first registered with Companies House, this was The Brewery On The Hill. You do wonder whether this would have become a global phenomenon had founder John Hickling not quickly changed the name to Vocation. Just eight years on, it's one of the hippest, most happening and inventive brewers around. Who could have predicted back then, that alongside Magic Rock, they would form in the Pennine foothills a perfect axis of craft beer supremacy?

Long-time beer obsessive John was a founding partner in Nottingham's Blue Monkey Brewery, and after stepping away from that, realised he missed the challenge and craft of brewing – and established the brewery in his new hometown of Hebden Bridge. Since then, punchy ales such as the dry-hopped **Bread & Butter** (3.9%), the intensely bitter session IPA **Heart and Soul** (4.4%) and the black IPA **Divide & Conquer** (6.5%) have struck a chord with drinkers both in the UK and on export to over 30 different countries.

Leeds design agency Robot Food established Vocation's obsession with the ampersand which lends itself well to catchy names like the American pale **Pride & Joy** (5.3%) and double IPA **Smash & Grab** (8%). A recent visit to the lovely Victorian Beer Cafe in Halifax afforded the opportunity to try out the cloudy straw-coloured **Hop Skip & Juice** (5.7%) whose big citric bite is given extra resonance by a determined prickle of carbonation.

A steady stream of investment has seen the arrival of 15 new fermenters, a yeast plant, whirlpool, and bottling line – in addition to a greater degree of automation in the brewery. Each played its part in

annual production heading somewhere north of ten million pints a year, in a period that has seen them extend from one industrial unit to three.

A new canning line installed just weeks into the pandemic allowed Vocation to increase capacity from 3,000 to 15,000 cans an hour, enabling a rapid switch from keg to packaged sales. "It arrived from Parma just as Covid began," said Matt. "Italy went into lockdown before us, so we had to hire engineers from around the world to get it up and running. That helped us to drive us to where we are now. We actually did really well out of Covid. We were perfectly set up, and didn't have to furlough a single member of staff. It's put us in a strong position to get throught the next few years."

Yet even while servicing these mass-market sales, Vocation's pursuit of innovation is relentless. They launched 78 new beers in 2021, some of them one-offs, collaborations and special editions, others which might edge their way towards the core range.

Sunset Overdrive (5.5%) is a pina colada sour, **Maple Glaze** (6.8%) a maple and coconut stout. The phenomenal **Mint Chocolate Stout** (12.2%), given firm body and mellow character through nine months in bourbon casks, is part of a new barrel-ageing programme. Matt, whose CV includes Bass in Tadcaster, Leeds Brewery and Manchester's Marble, shows me their vast store of 550 wooden barrels, which have previously held everything from Sauvignon Blanc to maple syrup. "We tend to put sour beers into wine casks, while sweeter, bolder ones go into whisky and bourbon ones. Occasionally we have the arduous task of tasting them – deciding which are ready, which need to age for longer, and which might be blended.

"This is my favourite," says Matt, handing me a glass of the chocolate and cherry stout **Imperial Kirsch** (11%). "It's genuinely wonderful. We do the mainstream beers of course, but when we do things like this, we can be as good as anyone in the world." His talents were recognised with the Brewers Journal Brewer of the Year award in 2021.

This commitment to the new, the experimental and the interesting seems hardwired into the Vocation DNA. In a recent update from the brewery, owner John Hickling said: "Each new beer involves refining a recipe, sourcing the ingredients, and designing a new label from scratch. It's a lot of work, but we do it because we never want to lose touch with the creativity and innovation that got us here in the first place."

The Vocation story looks set to run and run. And as John says: "It's hard to believe that only a few years ago, it was just me and the dog."

🍺 **Life & Death** (6.5%)

Despite its strength, forbidding name, and Gothic stylings of the label, this is actually a very accessible beer, a full-bodied cloudy premium IPA whose pineapple aroma and mango, grassy notes lend a lovely sweet softness that dulls the sharp, angular notes of its prodigious hop content. Small wonder that it remains Vocation's biggest seller, amounting for around a third of production. The juicy, unashamedly murky **Love & Hate** (7.2%) takes this experience a stage further.

Wensleydale Brewery

Unit 4, Badger Court, Leyburn, DL8 5BF; T: 01969 622463;
W: wensleydalebrewery.co.uk; E: geoff@wensleydalebrewery.co.uk;
🄵 *@wensleydale_brewery;* 🄳 *@wensleydale_ale*

Friends Geoff Southgate and Carl Gehrman started working at the brewery in Carlton while still at school; when they took over in 2013 they were two of the youngest brewery owners in the UK at 23 and 22 respectively. 2018 saw the friends expand into new premises five miles away in Leyburn. When I called in in March 2023, plans were already in hand for a summer party to mark the tenth anniversary of the takeover.

There's much to celebrate, as production continues to grow, with a new fermentation tank added last year and another on order, extra staff – and a growing reach that remains founded in knowing their customers. "We used to concentrate on the Dales but now we deliver everywhere from Tyneside to Doncaster, the east coast to the Lancashire border," says sales boss Miles Laprell. "Doing it ourselves means that we can rack the beers in the cellar, and deal with any issues or questions that licensees might have. That kind of customer service is vital to a small brewery like ours."

The overwhelming majority of Wensleydale's production goes into cask and is based around a tight core range that includes **Black Dub** (4.4%), a luxuriant, silky smooth oatmeal stout, packed with roasty chocolate tastes and named after a deep, dark pool near ruined Middleham Castle. **Falconer** (3.9%) delivers distinct orange character and there's a courteousness to the way the 4.5% **Wensleydale Gold** treads gingerly across the palate, though some firm bitterness quickly asserts itself, buzzed around by significant carbonation. The aftertaste leaves a significant dryness in the back of the throat.

But these are eclipsed by the pleasant and easy-drinking bright pale ale **Semer Water** (4.1%) whose aroma transmits pronounced gooseberry which joins forces with apple and lemon in a bitter refreshing taste. "It sells more than the others put together. Nearly every pub in the Dales has it," says Miles. "But our customers, particularly in Leeds, York and

Newcastle, are always after something different, and so we brew a new beer every week." Most are of sessionable strength: "The biggest-sellers in that market are 4%-plus," says Miles – so the rich and dangerous **Nightshade Imperial Stout** (10%) must be something of an aberration. Less challenging is the dry, milky-yellow IPA **What You Want** (5.2%) which shows the talents of the ubiquitous Mosaic hop. Alternate brews do the same with Citra. The stronger **Protagonist** (6.4%) takes that rich and oily IPA experience to the next level.

The brewery logo, a majestic shield with a sweeping sash and magnificent Bolton Castle in two-tone silhouette, speaks of the Yorkshire heritage and tradition this brewery is proud to uphold.

 **Gamekeeper** (4.3%)

Over several years I've led the judging for the beer category of the Flavours of Herriot Country awards – and this was the 2018 winner. It shimmers a deep translucent russet in the glass, with a tranquil caramel aroma, before treating the palate to a moreish malty lathering of pillowy comfort. It is as genial and avuncular as you would expect a gamekeeper to be, yet its strength is just enough to flex the full-bodied muscle he might need to deal with some troublesome poacher or frustrated Lady of the Manor. In the aftertaste some grassy notes emerge – and you soon find yourself reaching for another.

Westgate Brewery

c/o HB Clark, Unit 1, Headways, Stanley, Wakefield, WF3 4FE; W: hbclark.co.uk

HB Clark of Wakefield is the UK drinks trade's largest independent wholesaler, a business which continued uninterrupted during the 1960s and 70s when the explosion of keg beer saw production in their own city centre brewery halted. A new micro-brewery resumed brewing in 1982 – and along with a host of other products, Clarks delivered their beers to 5,000 on-trade customers across the UK.

Though the brewery is now closed – and production seems to have shifted to Castle Eden in Durham – beers are still marketed under the Westgate name. Flagship products include the interestingly spicy **Classic Blonde** (3.9%) and sessionable **English Pale** (4%).

Wetherby Brew Co

York Road Estate, Wetherby, LS22 7SU; T: 01937 584637;
W: wetherbybrewco.com; E: info@wetherbybrewco.com;
🅕 🅧 🅘 *wetherbybrewco*

Great beer starts here

Wetherby's on-site taproom

"I'm pleased to say that we've weathered the Covid storm," says director John Fergusson of this fine micro which was established in 2017 in a former printworks a short walk from Wetherby town centre.

"Actually we are more of a nanobrewery," says John. Recent investment in a new brewkit may have tripled capacity, but at just 700 litres, Wetherby Brew Co remains among the region's smaller commercial brewers. "During lockdown, we launched a 'bag-in-box' and mini-keg range through a new web shop, and offered both national delivery and 'click-and-collect' orders. Being very small enabled us to adapt very quickly to challenges in the market."

Now on the other side of the pandemic, Wetherby is thriving: "Our turnover is higher than in the pre-Covid period.

"More recently we have developed our core range and we have also started packing in KeyKeg, including a new dry-hopped beer, **High Hopes** (5.2%)."

John previously had a hand in the launch of the excellent Quirky's in Garforth, and – just as there – Wetherby concentrates its efforts on traditional beers of sessionable strength. There's a gentle, slightly lemony **Blonde** (4%), a **Gold** (4%), an **IPA** (4.4%) and a coffee-ish **Porter** (4.3%) and a traditional easy-drinking, sparingly hopped **Bitter** (3.8%).

With its constantly changing range of in-house and guest beers, an on-site taproom is the ideal place to browse the range; street food and live music also continue to draw the punters. Nearly 300 have tried their hands as brewers in the company's 'Brewing Experience' sessions.

"There are obviously lots of other challenges on the horizon," says John. "But hopefully our combination of passion, hard work and flexibility – plus great beer – will get us through!"

Wharfe Beer

c/o Hambleton Brewery, Melmerby Green Rd, Melmerby, Ripon, HG4 5NB;
T: 01765 640108; E: office@hambletonbrewery.co.uk

The sad closure of Wharfebank Brewery in 2016 robbed the Yorkshire scene of one of its better small breweries.

From his premises in Pool-in-Wharfedale, boss Martin Kellaway and his brewers had established a good reputation for some exceptional ales in both cask and bottle, of which my own favourite was the cracking traditional Yorkshire dark bitter **Camfell Flame** (4.4%). Each gained a reputation in the local market; an expansion into the pub scene gave Martin the opportunity to showcase all his beers on a single bar, notably at the Half Moon in Pool, close to the brewery.

Two of these beers have been given a fresh lease of life at Hambleton Brewery. But for loss of "bank" from the title, the packaging seems unchanged – and a tasting of **Tether Blond** (4.1%), confirmed that the quality is undiminished. It retains its fruity, zesty character which begins with some tropical fruit in the aroma before some rounded caramel sweetness emerges and a really dry finish. It's a session ale of depth, substance and character. **Yorkshire IPA** (5.1%) is a classic regional take on this ancient style.

Wharfedale Brewery

16, Church Street, Ilkley, LS29 9DS; T: 01943 609587;
W: wharfedalebrewery.com; E: info@wharfedalebrewery.com;
@wharfedalebrewery; @wharfedalebeer

There have been several breweries with this name over the years – the first dating back to the late 1700s. So it's perhaps appropriate that the quaint, stone-flagged and 300-year-old Flying Duck in the town centre is the best place to appraise the produce.

This latest iteration of the brewery was set up in 2012 and remains rather in the shadow of its longer-established neighbour Ilkley Brewery.

Beers include the refreshing, palate-cleansing **Blonde** (3.9%) whose blend of New Zealand and American hops creates some lingering citrus and grapefruit notes. English hops and a blend of malts combine in the soothing floral session bitter **Best** (4%). Cascade and Citra hops both drive the zesty tropical flavours of **Citra** (4.2%) while plum flavouring gives a balance to the dark and well-rounded **Porter** (5%).

Wharfedale IPA (5.5%)

For me this is the standout beer from this great core range – and it's not simply because it's the strongest. A cocktail of Mosaic, Simco, Nelson Sauvin, Citra, Comet and Equinox hops combine to produce an easy drinking and smooth IPA which delivers fresh lemon and grapefruit flavours from the first whiff of the aroma through to the last knockings of the aftertaste.

White Rose

7 Doncaster Road, Mexborough, S64 0HL; T: 0114 2466334

2018 saw White Rose move out of Sheffield to new premises and a seven-barrel plant which produces ales such as the pale and gently bitter **Autumn Gold** (4.2%), more assertive **Winter Rose** (5%) and fruity Christmas ale **Snow Business** (4.2%).

Whitby Brewery

East Cliff, Whitby, YO22 4JR. T: 01947 228871; W: whitby-brewery.com; E: info@whitby-brewery.com; 🇫 🇩 *@whitbybrewery*

Established in a tiny plant in 2013, Whitby Brewery expanded a few years ago, relocating to a hand-built 20-barrel brewery and micropub in the shadow of Whitby Abbey on a rugged headland overlooking the North Sea, where the shadow of Stoker hangs heavy in the air. The core range is available in both cask and bottle: the zesty and refreshing light ale **Abbey Blonde** (4.2%), toffee and liquorice-accented porter **Jet Black** (4.5%), full-bodied ruby ale **Saltwick Nab** (4.2%) and the passion fruit and grapefruity **IPA** (5.2%). **Black Death** stout has recently been uprated to a devilish 6.66%, and remains favourite on Whitby's twice-yearly Goth Weekends, when the town is overrun by black-clad seekers of darkness and Dracula.

🍺 Whaler (4%)

This hazy amber ale announces itself in appropriately dramatic fashion. Prising off the cap unleashes a riot of zestiness and you are almost expecting the cheek-sucking tang of an uber-hopped India Pale Ale. But once it arrives on the palate it shows a much softer and less bitter side, with some interesting toffee notes and a fruit character drawn from the peach and mango end of the spectrum rather than its lemon and grapefruit extremes. Yet there is depth and substance untypical of a beer of such moderate strength.

Wilde Child Brewing

Unit 5, Armley Rd, Leeds, LS12 2DR; T: 0113 2446549;
W: wildechildbrewing.co.uk; E: info@wildechildbrewing.co.uk;
🅵 *@wildechildbrewing;* 🐦 *@wildechildbeer*

"It seemed like the whole industry was imploding," says Keir McAllister-Wilde, looking back at the early days of lockdown. "We struggled and had to let all our staff go. It was really rough."

The Covid-19 pandemic came as an emergency stop, just as this imaginative, inventive brewery was really going places. Genre-busting beers like the **Bourbon Imperial Stout Instant Hobo** (9%) and the strawberry cheesecake **Forces Collide** (8.3%) had given Keir a reputation for the unusual. His beers had a strong following – whether in supermarkets, local pubs, or at the regular open days at the Armley Brewery.

"We were flying at the start of 2020," he says. "It has taken us more than three years to get back to where we were."

2023 sees two significant changes to the business model – first Keir has been joined in the business by his wife Christine, and second, they are concentrating for the first time on a core range of three beers.

For a brewery famous for embracing the new, these core beers are remarkably mainstream. **Resplendent Perspectives** (3.8%) is a delicate golden English blonde, built around traditional hops First Gold and Goldings, which layer some lemony, modestly bitter notes over a firm malty backbone.

There is more strident bitterness to **The Inevitable** (4.2%), a sessionable US-style IPA, whose stone fruit and citric character derive from a liberal dose of American hops Amarillo and Equinox. Perhaps the pre-pandemic Wilde Child is most evident in **Brownie Hunter** (4.9%), a chocolate fudge brownie stout that has been a popular part of their roster for a while.

Though these will be augmented by a changing host of alternatives, many available in the off-trade through a deal with Morrison's, Keir is clear where his priorities lie: "Cask is king for us right now. There has been a shift in tastes towards

traditional beers, so we are moving away from the high-ABV, high-intensity beers. Now more than ever we have noticed a real thirst for cask beers, because if it's looked after properly, it's a superior product."

The Stonegate pub chain has guaranteed a broad reach for Keir's cask ales, which now amount to around 60-70% of his output. Even so, the desire for novelty remains: "We're selling to a cyclical breed of people, particularly the 'beer-tickers'. They want to see different stuff on the bar all the time."

And Keir remains cautious about projections for the brewery into the future: There's nothing consistent about this industry – one month we might have a blinder, the next much less so. We're having to scrap around for business and it seems like I'm working three times as hard for half the money."

So the decision for Christine to give up her job as a quantity surveyor seems a curious one. "Yes, I know it sounds a bit mad," Keir admits. "But she's bringing in her skills to help drive the company forward.

"So we're completely family-owned – and of course we have 100% of the risk. But so far, it's continuing to give us the life that we want."

Wishbone Brewery

2A Chesham Street, Keighley, BD21 4LG; T: 01535 600412;
W: wishbonebrewery.co.uk; E: info@wishbonebrewery.co.uk;
f **y** **◎** @wishbonebrewery

The wishbone emblem on eye-catching diamond-shaped pump clips ensures brewer Adrian Chapman's products stand out on the bar. And there are plenty, many of them unfined and vegan friendly, including the session IPA **Nightstar** (3.7%). Hazy **Dassler** lager (4.2%) derives lime freshness from New Zealand's Motueka hop, while **Divination** (5.6%) is a significantly hopped dry and fruit-juicey American IPA.

DASSLER
Unfined — Unfiltered
NZ Helles Lager
Motueka
4.2%

Many of the beers which featured in the previous edition of this book are no longer with us, but they have been replaced by a vast list of regular beers along with two specials each month. Though some of his beers make their way into can and bottle, cask and keg remain Adrian's priority.

His mickey-taking pale cask ale **Pastiche** (3.7%) features three fashionable hop varieties and was developed in response to SIBA's efforts to provide a definition for craft ale. "It roughly proves the fact that to a certain extent the hops you use – or can get hold of if you have enough money – guide what beers get highly rated by drinkers," he told me. "It shows how fickle the market for in-vogue hop flavours is, when you could make two technically correct beers but the one with Citra, Simcoe and Galaxy will rate more highly."

DIVINATION
American IPA
ABV 5.6%

NIGHT STAR
Unfined with a natural haze
Mosaic + Ahtanum + Summit
Session IPA
ABV 3.7%

🍺 Zoikes (4.2%)

The name sounds like something Lord Snooty might exclaim in a moment of distress, and this wonderful American-influenced pale ale draws comic book levels of dry fruity bitterness from its cocktail of Columbus, Ekuanot and Mosaic hops. There are some crisp lemon notes to the aroma as this hazy golden ale settles beneath a substantial foaming head. The taste is packed with so much juicy fruit, grapefruit and orange pith that you might not guess at its sensibly sessionable strength.

ZOIKES
American Pale Ale
Columbus Ekuanot Mosaic
ABV 4.2%

Wold Top Brewery

Hunmanby Grange, Wold Newton, Driffield, YO25 3HS; T: 01723 892222; W: woldtopbrewery.co.uk; E: enquiries@woldtopbrewery.co.uk; 🟦 🟦 *@woldtopbrewery;* 🟦 *@woldtopbrew*

Wold Top Brewery was founded in 2003 by Tom and Gill Mellor on their 600-acre farm high on the Yorkshire Wolds – and is now run by their daughter Kate and husband, Alex Balchin. They use home-grown barley and water gently filtered by Wolds chalk and drawn from the farm's own borehole. There is a focus on sustainability and maintaining biodiversity, and on sourcing ingredients and services as locally as possible.

Alex and Kate Balchin

The brewery supplies Yorkshire pubs with a range of year-round beers and two seasonal cask ales every month – and you'll find their bottles in the supermarkets too. Fragrant **Wold Top Bitter** (3.7%) is the entry-level ale, while others include the complex gluten-free **Marmalade Porter** (5%) and **Anglers' Reward** (4%), a refreshing pale ale with some quite perfumy aromas, biscuit and caramel, fruity bitterness and a lingering aftertaste.

Thankfully devoid of parsley, sage, rosemary and thyme, the excellent **Scarborough Fair** (6%) is a beautifully sparkling IPA with fruity aromas and a taste whose bitterness mellows into spicy vanilla and black cherry.

"The pandemic spurred us into launching bottle and mini-cask subscription offers, and online sales have boomed ever since," says Kate. "All these are certified gluten-free and we've found this to be a really popular market." Bottling their monthly specials for the first time, and pairing up with the Spirit of Yorkshire Distillery to create a range of barrel-aged beers, has further extended the choice for Wold Top's loyal customers.

211

The pandemic also saw the launch of the brewery's first lager, the cooling, soothing, herb, honey and lemon delight **Landmark** (4.2%). It has already garnered a string of awards including a gold medal at 2021's International Beer Challenge.

Gill sadly passed away in 2020 after a long battle with cancer while Tom has now retired. But the brewery they founded two decades ago continues to go from strength to strength.

Wold Gold (4.8%)

I picked up a couple of bottles of Wold Gold on a rambling trip to East Yorkshire. The occasion was our walking group's first ever trip to the Wolds, and we had an idyllic afternoon yomping through the gently-rolling fertile landscape, a day only marginally spoiled by me tumbling down a hill and barrelling headfirst into a tree.

I should have cracked open a bottle there and then; Wold Gold would make a perfect pick-me-up. Attractively clear yellow of colour, with a soft white head, the zesty aroma soon gives way to the soft and fruity taste of a lightly-carbonated beer that bathes the palate in bitterness and spice. The experience is completed by some interesting peaty earthy notes in a remarkable finish that last and lasts.

Woodland Brewing

14 Market Street, Penistone, Sheffield, S36 6BZ; T: 07894 532456;
E: woodlandbrewing@outlook.com; 🐦 *@woodlandsbrew*

It may have been innocently named after the dominant breed of local sheep, but Whitefaced was perhaps an ill-advised choice of name for a brewery.

The pandemic saw this changed to Woodland as the brewery shifted from a domestic garage to a nearby retail unit, from where brewer Dave Hampshaw produces a great range of ales, predominantly sold through their Penistone Tap and Brewhouse, which opened in 2020.

"Luckily we have managed to survive the last few years and even expanded the brewery," says Dave.

"As the hospitality market dried up we purchased a canning machine and moved all our production to small packs which we distributed locally, and served draught take-out in milk cartons!"

The taproom is an imaginative re-use of an unprepossessing shop unit, where beer barrels have been repurposed as seats and tables, while filament bulbs, strings of fairy lights and hop vines lend a little atmosphere to a convivial space.

A visit in spring 2023 afforded me the opportunity to try several of Dave's beers. **Beyond The Groves** (4.4%) is a crisp, clear and golden cask ale with a refreshing bite; the cloudy and pale-straw kegged **Reluctant Superhero** (4.1%) is packed with juicy mandarin and **What Goes Around** (4.8%) is a cloudy American pale. For me the standout beer was the stronger, big-bodied and slightly carbonated pale ale **Illusions** (5.4%), which has a hint of sweet caramel among the rich citric flavours, and departs with a big bitter aftertaste.

York Brewery

c/o Black Sheep, Wellgarth, Crosshills, Masham, HG4 4EN; T: 01765 689227; W: yorkbrewery.co.uk; 🆒 🐦 *@York Brewery*

It was a significant shock when the big-hitting York Brewery went into administration in 2018. Their beers were well loved and widely distributed; their small pub chain properly-kept and well frequented. Thankfully, Black Sheep was able to step into the breach and keep these great beers in the market, while also taking the opportunity to finally dip its toes into the pub-owning trade.

Crisp, dry and refreshing **Guzzler** is very much the session beer, whether it's the 4% version in bottle or the 3.6% brew which they send to the pubs. It's the essence of an easy-drinking pale ale, with a suggestion of tangerine in the aroma, a crisp blast of fresh fruit with a touch of carbonation and a slight buttery silkiness, before a dusty dryness emerges right at the finish, just tempting you to drink some more.

Yorkshire Terrier (4.2%) settles to a bright attractive golden colour, with a thinnish head that soon fritters away. There are some short-lived zesty notes to the aroma, but its true character really comes out on the palate where an appropriate, terrier-like bite and some easy carbonation unleash the autumnal crispness of apples and the soft reassurance of caramel.

Centurion's Ghost (5.4%) is a dark, smooth and mellow mild.

Though currently brewed in Masham, the search continues for the right premises to allow this much-loved brewery to return home.

Minster Ale (4.2%)

The medieval biblical tableaux of the Mystery Plays are an important part of the vivid tapestry that makes up this ancient city. Traditionally each of the play's 48 scenes was staged by one of the city's craft guilds; the local coopers who furnished brewers with wooden beer barrels were, perhaps appropriately, responsible for staging the *Fall of Man*.

The link between brewing and the ecclesiastical life of the city continues through this zesty flaxen ale, slightly effervescent, yet packed with more genuine fruity, hoppy bitterness than you might expect from an ale of such modest strength. The aroma has suggestions of cider, but peach and apricot take over once it hits the palate, before a long significant aftertaste rounds off a wholly splendid experience.

Yorkshire Brewhouse

Goulton St, Hull, HU3 4DD; W: yorkshirebrewhouse.com; T: 01482 755199; E: brewery@yorkshirebrewhouse.com; 🟦 *@yorkshirebrewhouse;* 🟦 *@yorkshirebrewho*

A conversation between two friends at a Hull FC game had immediate consequences: "We were drinking a really poor mass-produced keg beer, and thought 'we can do better than this'," says co-founder Simon Cooke.

Before the evening was out they had bought a 200-litre brewkit on eBay, and before long were brewing in the ground-floor warehouse of Simon's long-established IT business. Having upscaled to a 500-litre kit, Simon now creates 13 different beers which are split roughly 50-50 between cask and bottle and can be found in pubs and off licences around Humberside. A webshop brings in a further stready stream of orders.

Simon Cooke

A lover of Black Sheep and Timothy Taylor, Simon admits that his best bitter **Ey-Up** (4%) is as close as he can get to these Yorkshire legends. Even so, the light amber ale **Reet** (3.8%) is his sessionable big-seller.

With its black and white stylings, the smoky **Faithful** stout (4.7%) honours the rugby league club that played such a key role in Yorkshire Brewhouse's foundation. Being more naturally a Rhinos supporter, I wasn't pre-disposed to this one, but it won me over. There are some gentle milk chocolate notes to the aroma, and though these persist into the taste they are soon supplanted by bigger flavours, acrid woodsmoke, peat and bitter coffee. Even so, after that first shock of its assault, it soon settles to a substantial, hearty soporific.

Initially naming his India Pale Ale **YPA** caused Simon a minor skirmish with those nice chaps at Rooster's who already brewed one under the same name. The dispute was settled amicably – Yorkshire Brewhouse were permitted to sell everything they had already badged, before adding an E, to denote its East Riding roots. **EYPA** (3.9%) is a lovely, light and refreshing pale.

"Micropubs want something different all the time," says Simon. "So often we take the same core beer and flavour it differently, so we've used additions like coffee in our stout." **Tenfoot** (3.9%) is a further case in point, a more floral version of the EYPA.

"We're still selling everything that we brew," says Simon. "But we're being quite selective about where we send it to." And should the need ever arise to increase volume, a 4,000-litre kit, picked up when Great Heck brewery went under, is poised and ready to be churned into action.

 **Hull of a Brew** (3.6%)

As occasionally happens in brewing, a happy accident spawned a wonderful new beer. "I was trying to brew a porter but got all the measurements wrong," says Simon. "This was supposed to be rich and dark." It's neither, a rich bright copper colour with only a modest body, and with its easy-drinking nature, gentle toffee malty taste and sessionable strength an almost perfect example of a crafted Yorkshire mild.

Yorkshire Coast Brewery

The Funny Onion, 105 Hilderthorpe Road, Bridlington, YO15 3ET;
W: yorkshire-coast-brewery.com; E: customers@yorkshire-coast-brewery.com

Head brewer Steve Golden led Bradford's Trough Brewery for many years, and was a fix-it consultant for lots of others before establishing Yorkshire Coast Brew Co in the basement of the Funny Onion. Though that pub is now closed, the brewery website suggests the beers are still available at the Yorkshire Tap in nearby Bridge Street.

Yorkshire Dales Brewing Company

Abbey Works, Askrigg, DL8 3JT; T: 01969 622027;
W: yorkshiredalesbrewery.com; E: rob@yorkshiredalesbrewery.com;
f @yorkshiredales.brewery; ✖ @yorkshiredalesb; ⊙ @yorkshiredalesbrewery

Over almost two decades, brewer Rob Wiltshire has created hundreds of different brews – cask, unfiltered craft keg and bottle-conditioned – each with its own unique recipe. His success has seen the beers distributed widely across Yorkshire and an export deal to Germany, while a move from his original converted milking parlour into new premises has created a new American-influenced microbrewery experience.

Several of the permanent beers reflect that influence, including the assertively citric American session ale **Butter Tubs** (3.7%), peachy **Nappa Scar** (4%), helles-style **Muker Silver** (4.1%) and **Askrigg Ale** (4.3%), an IPA whose big flush of tropical fruit is derived from Amarillo hops. Two more traditional British beers, the brown ale **Askrigg Bitter** (3.8%) and dark mild **Drover's Arms** (3.9%) complete the regular catalogue.

The strictures of lockdown saw Rob and wife Anne establish a beer garden at the brewery; the recent addition of a weekend taproom at the site means they can now welcome drinkers, whatever the weather.

Garsdale Smokebox (5.6%)

Smoky rauchbiers originated in Germany. Legend tells us that a brewhouse survived a fire at Bamberg's medieval cathedral in Northern Bavaria, but the malt had been exposed to the smoke, creating a novel beer which remains popular with tourists and locals alike.

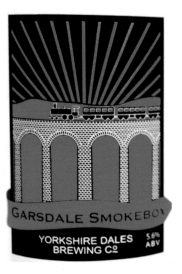

To ensure authenticity, Yorkshire Dales Brewing imported malt from Bamberg which had been dried over open fires made from beechwood logs. Sometimes native rauchbiers can be too extreme, too packed with acrid smoke that any nuance of flavour is choked out of the brew. But here we find a lighter touch that lets all those flavours breathe.

The smoke is unmistakeable all the same. As you prise off the cap you are struck with bonfire flavours, black treacle, fireworks and perhaps a whiff of cordite in a jet-black beer with a thin ivory head.

While this sense of the dark days of autumn is maintained on the palate, the influence of sweet sherry, black cherries and dark chocolate can also be sensed in a brew which would provide an interesting counterpoint to Wensleydale's moist and crumbly cheese.

Hops are doubtless used somewhere in the brew, yet their influence is dialled right down in a bottle-conditioned beer of substance, strength, practically zero bitterness and very little carbonation.

Yorkshire Heart

The Vineyard, Pool Lane, Nun Monkton, York, YO26 8EL; T: 01423 330716; W: yorkshireheart.com; E: sales@yorkshireheart.com; *@yorkshireheartvineyard;* *@yorkshire_heart*

With a cider press added to its vineyard and brewery, Yorkshire Heart has most of the major booze options covered; a popular visitor centre has enhanced its reputation as a top tourist attraction.

The name is ripe for beery puns, which include the smooth and coffee-ish mild **Darkheart** (4%) and the chestnut brown toffee-ish session ale **Hearty Bitter** (3.7%). **Silverheart** (4%) is a moderately-bitter, crisp and bright, pale golden effervescent IPA.

In recent years some new brews have been added to the range, alongside a refresh of the design. **Ghost** (5.4%) is a smooth and significantly chocolatey porter, **Liberty** (5%) a punchy, spicy lager.

This full-bodied liquoricey **Blackheart Stout** (4.8%) looks absolutely perfect – impenetrably jet-black, with a firm ivory head that retains its shape as the level falls. There is some attractive dark chocolate to the aroma, and on the palate it provides a wispy smokiness and a silky, luxurious layering of sweet vanilla and tobacco.

Off The Wheaten Path (3.5%)

Malt is a key ingredient of the brewing process, and though some beers are brewed with malt from naturally gluten-free cereals such as rice or maize, the overwhelming majority use barley malt, which introduces gluten to the recipe from the start. To market a beer as gluten-free, brewers must then break down the gluten, usually using an enzyme to reduce its presence in the finished product. Only once it is at trace levels, below 20 parts per million, can the 'gluten free' designation be attached, and even so, the list of allergens must state that barley was used in the process.

To anyone not on a gluten-free diet, the key test remains in the quality of the beer. And this is second to none – a beautiful clear golden ale, with some appley zest in the aroma, leading to a complex citric taste of bitter grapefruit and lemons, and more refreshing fruit character than its modest strength would ever suggest. Nice name too.

Zapato Brewery

Holme Mills, Slaithwaite Road, Marsden, HD7 6LS; T: 01484 521954;
W: zapatobrewing.com; E: info@zapatobrewing.com;
🅕 🅧 @zapatobrew; 🅘 @zapatobrewery

Beer consultant Matt Gorecki, a big noise behind beer festivals in Manchester and Leeds, cut his teeth with North Bar group before establishing his own cuckoo brewery, using spare capacity at Northern Monk, Kirkstall and Atom – and named after Mexico's anarcho-leftist Zapatistas. Now installed in a former textile mill west of Huddersfield, Matt has an attractive taproom and beer garden to the front and a brewery to the rear. It's here that he's established his core range on home soil, and taken the opportunity afforded by his own brewkit to experiment.

He offers drinkers plenty of choice. The crisp **Pico de Pinto** (3.2%) is a simple cleansing table beer, designed as the accompaniment to a Neapolitan pizza, while blackberries and raspberries add colour and just a gentle tartness to the **Beaucoup Weiss** (3%).

Double Zero (4%) is "our steady away pale ale," says Matt; part of each brew will go into cask. He describes export-style porter **Doom** (6%) as a "base beer" to which he can add flavourings depending on his mood – iterations have included a black bean version, one made with liquorice, and another with honey and grape molasses.

Whatever Whatever (10%) is a robust, assertive coffee and chocolate stout, packed with flavour and substance, yet never venturing too far into sweetness.

Naturally-fermenting saisons and fruit beers, and an ever-changing choice of IPAs all offer further proof of a fervent imagination and a brewery bursting with promise.

🍺 **Zapatapale** (5.5%)

Citra hops form the backbone of this chunky, big-bodied pale ale, though the precise character of the beer changes with different dry-hopping recipes at each brew. The version unveiled in the cloisters of Kirkstall Abbey during 2022's Leeds International Beer Festival frothed exuberantly, throwing off zinging zesty aromas; grapefruit and lemon dominated on the palate, held together with some gentle malt.

Gone but not forgotten

The list of breweries lost in the past four years is shockingly long, and includes some who were much loved and respected – the likes of Great Heck, Hop Studio, Bad Co, Revolutions and Naylors in Cross Hills. December 2022 saw the closure of Linfit, which had graced Linthwaite's Sair Inn for almost 40 years. Mexborough's Concertina Brewery – which had the distinction of being featured in renowned beer writer Roger Protz's *300 Great Beers to Try Before You Die* – is no more.

We've lost Beer Monkey, Cap House, Cathead, Crosspool and the Crafty Little Brewery; Geeves, Gene Pool, Ghost and Golcar; Vadum, Old Vault and Korrupt'd; Partners and Penistone; Five Towns and Three Valleys.

Some have upped sticks. Three Peaks has taken its Yorkshire name to Lancashire. Don Valley has gone to Lincolnshire, Treboom to Wales. Legends Keith and Sue Simpson closed Brown Cow Brewery to take a well-earned retirement.

Some closures may be temporary. Lazy Turtle Brewing is finding new premises, Henry Smith is in transition. Long-standing breweries at the New Inn in Cropton and Fox and Newt in Leeds were also both out of operation.

Hopefully some of the good folk behind these businesses will take renewed strength from the positive stories of others who have fought back, and will themselves find a way to return to the bar.

Acknowledgments

While it's my name on the cover, a book like this can only be a collaborative effort, and I'm grateful for the assistance I've received from numerous sources. A special mention must once again go to CAMRA stalwart and author Dave Pickersgill, whose expertise on breweries from around the Sheffield area is second to none. His new edition of *Sheffield's Real Heritage Pubs* is well worth a read.

I'm grateful to John Hartley of the Halifax and Calderdale Branch of CAMRA, for his knowledge of breweries in the area, and specifically for his help in updating the entries on Eagle's Crag and Stod Fold. Andrew Heyes lent similar support with the entries from the Bradford area.

Thanks also to my wife Katrina for accompanying me on numerous visits to breweries, making endless cups of coffee during my long writing sessions, and putting up with my endless requests to 'try this beer'.

Thanks to all those others who have helped with the arduous task of tasting these beers and sharing their opinions. They include Jake Shipley, Ben Jenkins, Gareth Dunworth, Jonathan Davies, Steve Dudman and Andrew Hayes.

Photography

Many of the images are my own, and others have been kindly supplied by the breweries. But thanks to the following who also supplied photographs for use in the book: Mark Newton (Abbeydale), Nancy Anne Harbord and Sam Wilson@Buca (Anthology), Dave Pickersgill (several, including True North, Brew Social and Dead Parrot), Christopher Manson (Pumphouse and Wold Top). The photographs of Ilkley Brewery are by Xanthe Hutchinson (p6 and p95), Laura Mate (p96) and Beershots (p97 top).

I'd also like to give a special thank you to German beer writer Markus Raupach for his images from Northern Monk, North Brewing, Samuel Smith's and Triple Point.

IT'S THE BEER TALKING

A walk with the author

Yorkshire Beer Bible author Simon Jenkins hosts regular walking tours in Leeds, where you can learn about some local history and heritage – and call in for drinks at one or two of his favourite pubs. Visit the website itsthebeertalking.co.uk or scan the QR code for details of forthcoming events.